Vespers

Vespers

Contemporary American
Poems of Religion
and Spirituality
Edited by Virgil Suárez and
Ryan G. Van Cleave

University of Iowa Press

Iowa City

University of Iowa Press, Iowa City 52242
Printed in the United States of America
http://www.uiowa.edu/uiowapress

The publication of this book was generously
supported by the University of Iowa Foundation.

Printed on acid-free paper

Library of Congress
Cataloging-in-Publication Data
Vespers: contemporary American poems of religion
and spirituality / edited by Virgil Suárez and Ryan G.
Van Cleave.
      p.   cm.
   Includes bibliographical references and index.
   ISBN 0-87745-855-3 (pbk.)
   ISBN 0-87745-875-8 (cloth)
   1. Religious poetry, American.   2. American
poetry—21st century.   3. American poetry—20th
century.   4. Spiritual life—Poetry.   I. Suárez, Virgil,
1962–   .   II. Van Cleave, Ryan G., 1972–   .
PS595.R4V47 2003
811'.6080382—dc21   2003041003

03 04 05 06 07 C 5 4 3 2 1
03 04 05 06 07 P 5 4 3 2 1

It is always an invisible belief that sustains the edifice of our sensory world and deprived of which it totters.

MARCEL PROUST

I am willing to leave God out of the matter, since I personally find no words to qualify or invoke that Name. But I am unwilling to leave spirit out, spirit . . . as much an issue of nihilism as of belief. A great writer may deny meaning to spirit—witness Kafka, Beckett—but we think it vulgar and vapid if he do so without trace of despair; and we note how often he returns to deny.

IHAB HASSAN

Contents

Editors' Note

Poetry is an endeavor of creating expectations and either fulfilling or denying them. As we were sorting through thousands of poems in the organizational stages of our previous anthologies, *American Diaspora: Poetry of Displacement* and *Like Thunder: Poets Respond to Violence in America*, we knew on some level that we were creating the expectation that beyond pointing out and speaking of the many issues in these two books, we might offer a sense of peace, of closure, of redemption. In looking back at *American Diaspora* and *Like Thunder*, we realized that we needed to go further, to show a way out, one road to hope, an opportunity for meaning.

Thus we saw the need for this anthology—a meditation on who, what, and why we are. Perhaps it was there all along, waiting for us in our previous anthologies, our own poetry, our own lives.

We solicited many of the best poets in America and added to their selections some from our own reading, and before long, word of mouth had spread and we had boxes of poems ranging from deathbed spirituals to initiation songs, from transformative epics to transcendent sonnets. At the root of every religion is the premise that an individual can connect profoundly with a reality that's somehow beyond the personal, limited self and yet part of it as well. For us, the poems that we finally chose spoke most clearly to that connection individually and collectively and thus demanded inclusion. Always we sought poems with their own underlying music, but we never lost sight of our goal: assemble as many accessible religious/spiritual-based poems as possible that exhibit the courage, the range, and the passion that infuse the landscape of contemporary American poetry with so much collective energy.

The Romanian American anthropologist of religion, Mircea Eliade, proposed that the best way to understand world religions is to examine their cosmologies, meaning their views of both how the world came into being and how it operates on a daily basis. Many of the poems here do exactly that. A number of these poems also address ideas that are central to many spiritually profound issues:

the meaning of life, the relationship of humankind to the divine, the existence of evil and suffering, and death, to name just a few. Many of these poems delve into the theodicy problem, which seems more relevant today than ever, after events like Waco and Columbine and perhaps the most important event in the last fifty years of American history, the September 11 tragedy.

How *does* one reconcile the idea of a benevolent and all-powerful deity with the suffering and evil that seem an inherent part of human existence? How can an investigation of the sacred—in prayer, in song, in poetry—help move us into a better understanding of the most intimate of encounters, the personal self meeting the cosmic self?

In *A Poetry Handbook*, Mary Oliver writes: "These days many poets live in cities, or at least in suburbs, and the natural world grows even more distant from our everyday lives. Most people, in fact, live in cities, and therefore most readers are not necessarily very familiar with the natural world. And yet the natural world has always been the great warehouse of symbolic imagery. Poetry is one of the ancient arts, and it began, as did all the fine arts, within the original wilderness of the earth. Also, it began through the process of seeing, and feeling, and hearing, and smelling, and touching, and then remembering." The connection between the natural world and the inner lives we lead as poets can help keep us whole, sound, complete. As the poems began to pour in, we realized that this was one of the central issues developing a life of its own, not just in this book but in contemporary American poetry.

More so than other cultures, Americans have a distinct anxiety over occupational and vocational calling that stems from our Puritanical heritage. We have an anti-intellectual preference for experience and individualism over theory. We have a bias against ritual. It's part of who we are, and in seeing how some of our best writers tackle these challenging ideas and philosophies, we can come to a better understanding of who, what, and why we are.

We didn't give much guidance to poets as we requested work and finally put the general call for submissions out. We simply gave them the title, *Vespers: Contemporary American Poems of Religion and Spirituality*, and the loose idea that the book would be more than a creative exploration of theological concerns, but rather a roadmap of where we've been, where we are, and where we're headed in terms of our spiritual/religious literacy and existence. Our intention was to let the poets and the poems themselves show us the way. And they did so, to wondrous effect.

This collection of rich and resonant poetry—led by Pulitzer Prize winners Stephen Dunn and Carolyn Kizer and backed up with many familiar names and perhaps a few worthy yet unfamiliar ones as well—will keep you company, and will be good company, whatever your own spiritual/religious background is or will be. This book can save your life or the life of someone you know. In echoing the thoughts, concerns, and fears that linger in our souls, we realize that we're not alone, that we're never truly alone, that even in the face of darkness the world is unsilent, beautiful, and joyous.

The words in these poems are our daily bread. Have your fill today, and come back again and again, as needed.

Acknowledgments

We would like to thank our families for providing much-needed support during the years we spent compiling and editing this book. Our sincere thanks and heartfelt gratitude to the good folks at the University of Iowa Press for believing that this project was as important as we knew it was and for offering us much-needed encouragement and support. Also, and mostly, a giant thank you to all the wonderful writers who were generous not only in sharing with us their great work but also for helping us contact and solicit more work from kindred souls. Finally, we would like to thank the owners and staffs of Samrat's and Gordo's, where we spent the better part of two years with our laptops, devouring Cuban sandwiches, curry chicken, empanadas, and cup upon cup of high-octane coffee and cafecitos.

This book is dedicated to all those whose lives are engaged with Mystery.

Mercy

Small flames afloat in a blue duskfall, beneath trees
anonymous and hooded, the solemn trees—by ones
and twos and threes we go down to the water's level edge
with our candles cupped and melted onto little pie-tins
to set our newest loss free. Everyone is here.

Everyone is wholly quiet in the river's hush and
    appropriate dark.
The tenuous fires slip from our palms and seem to settle
in the stilling water, but then float, ever so slowly,
in a loose string like a necklace's pearls spilled,
down the river barely as wide as a dusty road.

No one is singing, and no one leaves—we stand back
beneath the grieving trees on both banks, bowed but
    watching,
as our tiny boats pass like a long history of moons
reflected, or like notes in an elder's hymn, or like us,
death after death, around the far, awakening bend.

Heavenly

They are potted at night, pink, and packed
with mulch or peat, chert in handfuls at their base
for weight and hydration, they are red as day-
break is red breaking over the buildings,
they are flecked white, gray-white, and silver
like the quick sides of the sunfish that will
circle the shallow fountain all summer.
This morning I think even the afterworld
must be traced with geraniums, one block long,
for that is how far the city fathers
have gone, pot by pot, to pretty the town.
And what shall we do but admire them,

the fathers, who like their flowers have turned
fresh outheld faces to greet ours, and are
lined up in front of the drugstore, sub shop,
barbershop, the library, and fountain,
hair like little wings on the morning's breeze.
They wave to show us magnificent
flowers. Heavenly, our gift, these will bloom
clear through the summer. Let us praise them then
and stroke their soft leaves which will scent our hands
to pass on to all that we touch today—
for who are we to deny the next life,
having come far already, in this one.

The Puritan Way of Death

How hard this life is hallowed by the body.
How burdened the ground where they have hollowed it,
    where they have gathered to set the body back,

handful by handful, the broken earth of her.–
They have gathered to sift back the broken clod
    of her body, to settle her, now, back down.

"A child is a man in a small letter," wrote
John Earle in sixteen twenty-eight, "Natures fresh
    picture newly drawne in Oyle, which Time and much

handling dimmes and defaces," wrote Prof. David
E. Stannard, Yale, nineteen seventy-seven.
    A stutter of winter wind shakes the plain trees

until they seem, leafless, huddled over, to weep.
But John Earle was not a Puritan. Here then,
    at the grave of the girl who was sorely bitten

by the Small Pox, they do not bow down, neither
raise their heads, nor hold hands against the cold.
    This fruit of natural corruption and root

of actual rebellion both against God
and man must be destroyed, and no manner of
    way nourished . . . For the beating, and keeping down

of this stubbornness parents must provide
carefully, instructed John Robinson in
    the same year as Earle's *Micro-comographie.*

The frozen ground of their gaze steadies them.
The gray grasses shiver and snap at their feet.
    They do what they can. Long days and nights they
        stand

with her, through her fevers and ague, and clean her
gentle Vomit, and try to soothe the Pustules
    and her Eruptions, until there grow Hundreds,

and neither then a common poultice of Lint
dipt in the Variolous Matter, nor warmed
    Leaves of the Cabbage laid to her rapid heart,

nor prodigious bleeding, nor prayer, can save her.
They go astray as soon as they are born. They
    *no sooner **step** than they **stray**, they no sooner*

***lisp** than they **ly**,* mourns Cotton Mather, sixteen
eighty-nine. Yet he himself is father to
    fifteen, and loves them, suffering their afflictions.—

He sees in his *Lambs* in the *Fold* evidence
of God's love. Moreso His fury. *Are they **Young**?*
    *Yet the **Devil** has been with them already.*

At least, let us give thanks for a lease so short
that terror has short time to dwell. Only two
    of Mather's children live beyond their father,

as though a father's fealty be his children.
So the lamplighter takes up his grim vigil,
    torch in hand, and together we walk the slick path

through the centuries, where the ministers shall
say what has been said, what needs be repeated.
    Oh, blood upon the hands. Urine to the lips.

Let us burn the garments of disease lest they
cloak us now, and let our faith be provender,
    provision, and protection, and offer no

ly, no calumny, nor any words but these.
Let us stand before the door and gaze outward.
    Field and fallow. Fish and fowl. Mall and highway

now alike. She lives among us—. *She is ours,*
flesh of our flesh, whom our sorrows have begot.
    Let us walk beside ourselves with this grief, who

neither raise our heads nor hold hands to the cold.
She goes beside us, even so, even as
    I write this to you, neighbor, friend, daughter,

my reader, this day, in nineteen ninety-nine.
She reminds us always of this death, this life,
    which is redundant, awful, endless, and ours.

Les Mains du Bon Dieu
(after a line in Daigrepont's Cajun spiritual)

For my uncle, Ray Rougeau

The last word I can picture you saying to me
was "Faith." It sticks because you were never a man
people would call talkative, even before
the nurses wrote you down as unresponsive,
before they took your staring at the cracks
in the white walls of your room as some kind of loss.
They see in your eyes a man who would hand them back
anything they gave you without sign of recognition,
but every time you rest your eyes from the wall
to meet mine we are together on a popelier dock
in early fall, the sky flat-gray on the water.
A run of bull red has knocked the conversation
out of us, turning it all into cast and reel—
backbone and shoulders. The fish are so big
the only thing they hit is small crab
on shad rigs. We've already filled the boat
to near sinking, so you leave me there on the dock
to ride out our luck while you bring the first load
back to the camp to ice down. Alone, I live
a twelve-year-old's dream: every time I cast
I land a big one to pile on the dock as testament
to the day. It is more than I can handle, more
than we deserve, but I keep pulling them in.
You return in time to see my rod
arc and the line give more than it has all day.
You watch me fight this monster patiently
and load the boat again. Almost by script,
just when I want to fold, the fish runs
straight at us, between the pylons under the dock.
With no sign or pause you take the rod from my hand
and toss it into the water. It is all I can do
not to follow it, a rig worth more allowances

than I can imagine lost for one fish
in a pile of one hundred just like it. You pull me near
and whisper the word mostly to yourself. Your eyes
stare calmly at something just below the surface
I can not make out. When the redfish comes around
to make its last run at the gulf, the rod follows
as if delivered by the hands of God.
In a single motion you catch it up
and pass it to me to finish out the day.
Before my line breaks and your stare returns
to the wall, I have a sense of what you mean:
Mettez votre vie dans les mains du Bon Dieu.

The Hole in the Sea

It's there
in the hole of the sea
where the solid truth lies,
written and bottled,
and guarded by limp-
winged angels —
one word under glass,
magnified by longing
and by the light tricks
of the moving man
in the moon.
Nights, that word shows,
up from the bottle,
up through the water,
up from the imaginable.
So that all who cannot
imagine, but yearn toward,
the word in the water,
finding it smaller
in the hole in the sea,
rest there. If no one
has drowned quite
in the hole of the sea,
that is a point
for theology. "Blame God
when the waters part,"
say sailors and Hebrews;
blame God, who writes us,
from His holy solution,
not to be sunk,
though all our vessels
convey black messages
of the end of the world.
So goes the story,

the storybook story, so goes
the saleable story:
Courage is in that bottle,
the driest thing there is.

The Book of the Dead Man (#13)

1. About the Dead Man and Thunder

When the dead man hears thunder, he thinks someone is
    speaking.
Hearing the thunder, the dead man thinks he is being
    addressed.
He thinks he is being addressed because the sound
    contains heat and humidity—or groaning and salivation.
Isn't that always the way with passionate language—heat
    and humidity?
The dead man passes burning bushes and parting seas
    without inner trembling, nor does he smear his door
    with blood.
The dead man can only be rattled physically, never
    emotionally.
The dead man's neuroses cancel one another out like a
    floor of snakes.
He is the Zen of open doors, he exists in the zone of the
    selfless, he has visions and an ear for unusual music.
Now he can hear the swirling of blood beneath his
    heartbeat.
Now he can fall in love with leaves—with the looping lift
    and fall of love.
Naturally, the dead man is receptive, has his antennas out,
    perches on the edge of sensitivity to receive the most
    wanton prayer and the least orderly of wishes.
To the dead man, scared prayer isn't worth a damn.
The dead man erases the word for God to better
    understand divinity.
When nothing interferes, nothing interrupts, nothing
    sustains or concludes, then there's no need to separate
    doing from not-doing or to distribute the frequencies of
    the thunder into cause and effect.
The dead man speaks God's language.

2. More about the Dead Man and Thunder

The dead man counts the seconds between lightning and
thunder to see how far he is from God.
The dead man counts God among his confidants: they
whisper.
The dead man hears the screams of roots being nibbled by
rodents.
He notes the yelps of pebbles forced to maneuver and of
boulders pinned into submission.
He feels the frustration of bodily organs forced to be quiet.
He thinks it's no wonder the sky cries and growls when
it can.
The dead man's words can be just consonants, they can be
only vowels, they can pile up behind his teeth like
sagebrush on a fence or float like paper ashes to the top
of fathomless corridors, they can echo like wind inside a
skull or flee captivity like balloons that have met a nail.
The dead man serves an indeterminate sentence in an
elastic cell.
He hears a voice in the thunder and sees a face in the
lightning, and there's a smell of solder at the junction of
earth and sky.

Sounds of the Resurrected
Dead Man's Footsteps (#3)

1. Beast, Peach and Dance

He couldn't say it or write it or sign it or give it a name.

He was suffering, he was terrible, he had a shape you could
see in the fire.

He blamed the wine, God, the infamous events of
Bethlehem.

Each newborn appeared to him in the air, their gorgeous
proportions shaping the swaddling cloth each to
each.

On the one hand, he felt the galaxies cooling, the gears
clogging and the old passions frozen into debilitating
poses.

On the other hand, it was now April and he had a buzz on
because some seasons are their own nectar.

He could pick out a jacket and tie if he had to.

He could sit without twitching through the outdoor Mozart,
the band shell gleaming like a new star.

Around him, the concertgoers sat tight-lipped, their
expectations rewarded.

Before him, the night took on the sheen of flat glass and he
could see in it the beacons of the town, and the blue-
blackness of space just beyond.

His eyes fixed on a small, fuzzy star among many larger
stars.

He became obsessed with this star, certain it was a
Jewish star.

He felt that, if he could follow it, it would lead him to the
true story of Jesus.

That night, while Mozart resolved in the air, he began to
travel through time.

His small star would someday pass close to him but
not yet.

2. Angel, Portrait and Breath

The hands that were nailed, the ankles that were pierced as
   if one—he had seen such proclamations before, it being
   common.
The bodies that literally came unglued in the furnace, the
   bones festering in lye—he had seen the piles of coats
   and eyeglasses, there being many.
The same angel who watched over the crucified Jesus
   passed over the cremated Jews, or was that a cloud?
The smokestacks carried away their last breaths.
Then Jesus rose entire to show the power of belief.
The dead Jews disintegrated into earth, air and water to
   show the lasting effects of evil.
He could not give it a name but felt that night as if,
   whatever it was, it lived on a small star, encircled but
   apart.
Thereafter, ordinary objects displayed a consciousness of
   the presence of men and women.
The blackened pots and ladles of the kitchen appeared
   changed.
They shone from long years of sustenance, from soups and
   sauces.
And in the shop he felt it also in the saws and sawhorses, in
   the drop cloths and bent nails, each encrusted with the
   years.
In this manner, he came to see in common objects the
   shine of the angelic.
The divine and horrific were linked by things and their
   descendants.
It was possible to see the good and bad in a needle and
   thread, in a pencil and pad, in a spoon, in a shoe.
The cloud appeared to him by day and the little star by
   night.

Vision of Salt & Water
Elijah's horn

He dreamt that his ear was a small Africa.

His horn was a seismic instrument parting the water
in the boat that brought him here.

He played, superimposing the continent in his ear
to the soil beneath his feet, to reinvent the tired fire
of his mythology, to split the plum in the throat of
    the angel.

He pulled notes from the river. He parted the lips of
    the angel,
in his dream, searching the tongue with the original hand
for the ashes of its maker. He found only water, but he
was changed. He had become the water & slept with
the fingers of the angel in his mouth.

He played the air as if it were brass nipples of the
    saxophone
mutilating the lice that lay between the fire in his
    fingertips.

He designed a new sorrow in the circle of fifths
cutting his name into the lamb in the lung of the angel.

He set the landscape of the land where he was born on fire,
it did not burn but sweat the melody of its element
into a perfect sphere.

They, in the parallel water of the mutual dream, spilled out
    the formula
of the voice that formed the antique heart.

The angel asked Elijah if he knew the sound that would
    break
the lump of gold in the eternal breath & cut the blueprint
    in his vein
from the simultaneous.

Elijah paused, took the throne off his shoulder, away from
    his ear,
when it landed on the water it became the dirt at the foot
    of the door
in the angel's chest, his chest.

His face was in the water, the angel was in him.

*   *   *   *

He woke up humming the melody in the pearl
of his breath. He fingered the air playing the keys
like the breasts of a Siamese cat. The water flowed between
    his fingers
breaking the rhythm, disinfecting the small Egyptian
    wound in his pelvis
shaped like a flaw in the perfect rest. His skin sweat the
    feathers in his fury.

The sand in his cuticles had not been born there,
but rested on the floor of his rhythm, on & in the wet water,
burning the bridge of the journey into a million notes,
crushing the bird in the rose of his cranium.

The water was his wardrobe,
the angel his dresser, the water the gossip in the natural
    pitch.

Host

My father's body is the narrow grave
where they buried another man's heart alive.
Sometimes when he walks, he shakes a little,
unsure of the vital debt he carries.
When he pauses on the stairs, panting,

it is another man's flush he feels,
another man's sudden breath and shiver.
When he reaches for the words,
they come down just so far and wait.
The room he's in is another man's silence.

Some nights it burns at the center, this quiet
passing through him like a torch.
I worry naturally though for him
death is less than solitary,
less the dire property it was.

Every common kindness now, each warm meal
and paper cup of pills, is the unbroken
emblem of itself. At the root
of his pale throat is a gift,
a dark-red fruit too deep to harvest.

When he closes his eyes, he sees
the opening jaw of his ribs,
ravenous and steaming, taking in
the live bread. When the flesh goes vivid,
startled with blood,

it becomes the mourning tongue in his chest.
He could listen for hours lulled
by the faint sound on his pillow,
so distant there in the wet dark, his ear
pressed to the sternum of the world.

Transparencies

On a stone disk palette from ancient America
you see a carved hand with an eye in its palm,
flush with sight, awakened there to hold us to it,

and ringed about the rim an afflatus of snakes
coupled and fanged, tongues distended—they too are
    snakes—
so long they seem the body's lining blown inside out.

The whole mandala wavers as if the hand
were the mind's island lathered in fatal currents
and poison were its vitals, the crown of being

alert and abandoned to extremity's longing,
in the mortal book of skin we read our lives in.

*   *   *   *

If you look into the stone's tiny flecks of lime
and mica, you can still make out the faded stain
of flesh-paint, still conjure a spectacle of hands

that worked the surface with chisels and pigments,
that dipped their boar's hair brushes and tattoo needles
to illuminate the pages of their bodies, blood

rising to the color of blood, their skin littered
in a rash of eyes—less a second skin than a new
transparency, as if the needles made them more

permeable to one another's sight. The prick
of seeing grazed the stone, zeroed in from eye to eye.

*   *   *   *

When I first saw Christ with an eye in his hand,
it came as eerie comfort, to think he was less
alone out there, pinned to his cathedral wall,

his body pierced by the gazes of accusers.
It made me think of blood as light welling up
out of underworld rivers, or, if not light,

then the corporal mind that lets it in: red
as the wound's iconography and swoon, the desert
drink passed among thieves and untouchables,

the color of breaking forth, emergency red,
the fang's aftermath we relish and grieve.

* * * *

Pity the mind that feels charity for all mankind
and nothing but contempt for its neighbors.
Better to descend from the temples, to travel

the pipe-line of the throat like drink itself, down
the furnace of the shoulder, its anger and char,
the breastplate shivering like a railcar window,

through bruise-colored corridors to the world at hand.
So it was kindness looked out from darker reaches
of flesh, blind tissue awakened by the blind to see,

as if something broke the skin, some dream-legend
of literal palms surrendering their phantom gold.

* * * *

Any man's end has an eye at the center. Death
raises its giant hand and scoops back the body,
not lost exactly, but seeded in that ritual closure.

Never was flesh more the miracle-stranger,
never closer to the radiant gore of birth.
Out of the meaningless dirt, the palettes of stone.

We come to a place where even rocks have a face
and back, a name to forget. Even rocks keep watch.
Somewhere below, a corpse sheds its blaze of worms

as if earth had pierced the insensible
remains to light them on their solitary journey.

Durer's *Apollo*

When Durer drew Apollo, he placed him in a light-
er colored field surrounded by a golden
border. My friend Bill says it looks like a white kite,
this space the god stands in where he's shown holding
a happy sun. It is always morning here, flight
from morning some derivation of morning still; molten
noon, just morning terrified. We see what we might
call the lazy afternoon or advent of evening. Moldings
in our houses shift in dying light, a trick for our eyes
mostly. We even call dark *relief*, but Durer was in love
with this god. He works the god's gold in hair that lies
on his manly shoulders in the portraits, in the gloves
of buttery yellow he gives himself to wear, in the ties
gleaming on his blouse and coat, in *Great Turf*, groves,
bees. Radiant prayer, world where morning never dies.

Old Women Fishing from Bridges

There is something about dropping a line into the unseen.
Fishing we usually call it here. A mother fishes for clues
to her children's secretive lives in the piles of clothes
they relinquish to her for laundering. Another mother
occupies herself with other thoughts—too risky this
fishing. She might catch much more than she knows
what to do with. A boy fishes for the signals that keep
promising to add up to something. Another takes ends
of strings, all too willing to be the fish in these scenes.
He will let an Ariadne pull him out of the maze. Easy
work. He has only to respond to tug and taut in string.
Some fishermen don't know the first thing about waters
they fish in. Some girls fish with their eyes, use other
body parts when eyes don't work. The really bold cast
into the openness of heart, mind even. Some girls, boys
learn to fish in the wine market, on the tops of stoves.
My father-in-law liked the idea of having me in a boat
for whole afternoons. On the way out to *les Fordoches*
he pointed out the water moccasins sunning themselves
in the Spanish moss clusters overhead, thick black coils
in delicate gray nests. He pointed them out on fallen trees,
lying in the coffee-colored shallows at the front of his boat,
and the small alligators too sleeping in the mud flats near
the banks on either side. I saw to it that he liked the idea
only once. My mother sees fishing as the making of things.
Her table is full. The platters are steaming. Her children
are happy. My father and I filet our catches of sheephead,
redfish and speckled trout. We gut foot tubs of sac-a-lait,
bream. Fishing for my mother is an ichthyophagous dream.
But old women fishing from bridges fish mostly just
    for fish.

Penance and the Work Week

By Woundsday when a tongue-pierced Asian
girl left a note discreetly tucked thanking
for the hour and passion for Whitman,
by the time his accountant
chiseled Uncle Bill for another nine hundred,

by the time—didn't you just know it?—
he's licking at the glass
again, its cool eleven-year-old-casket-aged maple
sweet protection, soda spice, cubes nudging
lips like corrosive glaciers in a sea

of salvation, when bowed again
by authority, reloaded with indignation
behind a steaming barrel of pristine
plausible deniability, by then
his self-castration—head low, hoof shuffling

was one more ghost limping lost horizons.
Liars must have good memories, taught Quintinian.
The best part of Sundays, crevices
of recrimination where we creel so carefully,
best is they too pass as a dream.

Transport of the Dead

The only official method, of course,
is with scholar and priest always aboard.
Dead are lined symmetrically
onto shelves, then stacked in rows
as if on heavenly baking racks,
all feet pointing east.
A cross of holy water stripes each forehead,
a star each chin. A translucent wafer
is placed on each blue tongue.
The deads' hands are posed in an attitude
of grace, perhaps in anticipation of their
flight. Scripture and history's
data are chanted over the clatter
of ignited engines, and the ascent begins.

Of course, practical realities demand
that most transported dead
be loaded at night, tipped from dump trucks
in a tangle of faces and legs,
arms and charred feet
in a crazy gumbo, or like discarded figures
from a child's toy box. They are sprayed
with anti-odorant for the long trip
to the desert. Many officials
and editors of major periodicals know this,
and video was rumored
of a dock worker fanning a spray of urine
across bodies as he laughed with co-workers,
quote, "this'll preserve you bastards."
In either case, verified are
cargo planes the size of football fields,
the color of baked clay, wings marked
"Disaster Relief" in flawless Roman lettering.

The real truth, though, is that the legions
of dead are grotesquely under-reported
even at the highest levels.
Most never get off the ground at all.
They are burned where they lie, buried
under blankets of gravel. Priest
and scholar would never
let it rest, and what good
could that do the families, after all?
Why fan the flame? Let them have their rituals
and hallelujahs, leave alone those who sweat
for a living, who carry the weight
of secrets, of camels and angels and earth's molten core.

Christ, the End

As ghost I returned to them.

I ascended. They discovered only
shadows of their own grief,
heaved the stone away.

My wounds would not heal.
They wrapped me in coarse cloth.
I was limp when they lowered me from
that wooden crossroads.

Forgive them, I said.
Lightning rended the sky. Thunder.
Thieves recognized me.

Later he hanged himself, coins dropping
all over the darkness.
He is the one, called my most loved.
In the garden they came for me.

We laughed,
ate a fine dinner of fish,
loaves and figs, things of the good earth.
We shared common wine. Thirteen of us.

The town a miracle, streets of palms.
They sang in their rags.
The donkey, contrary beast, guiding me.

Forty nights.
The serpent whispered, but I dared not
answer. I scoured myself in sand.

I don't, my brother said. I don't,
I do not know him.

I threw the gold in their faces,
fatted ones deaf to the word.
You defame this house, I screamed.

The storm calmed.
These men, mine, cowered on deck.
I raised arms to clouds.
I awoke and came from below.

I took the bloodied face in my hands.
Which of you? I asked.
They rained stones down on her.

Lead us, they said.
A mangy group, fishermen and collectors.

The rest is known: I was a builder,
then a builder's apprentice.
The circumstances of my childhood
unnecessary.

Kings bowed. Goat and cow,
sheep, dove, the hard straw
my mother writhed upon.
My bemused and quiet father.

I descended.

No room, not for you,
leered the innkeep. His bolted door,
our knock, fearful. The beginning.

God

"God is in the high notes,"
the plane said, lowering
its landing gear.

"We like it when he
holds our hands,"
the children said

in the blue museum
where the Delacroix hangs
near the glass elevator.

"Tragic, the work of memory
erased like an answer
on an exam booklet."

"My ears have grown
disproportionately large."
"Tape them back in photos,"

suggested the saint.
"A fate most unkind,"
string said of the kite

found on the heath.
"In dreams she stays
for hours, and I don't

need Valium."
An important mood is waiting
for its sound bite to arrive.

"Through the keyhole
I could see his footwear.
I wouldn't call it oxblood."

"May I intrude?" he asked
of the storm. "Like a camera
or season, he registers

my face in increments
of shadow that dissolve
when they're arranged,"

said the shadow self-
importantly. "If then,
therefore, we regard

her March, April, May
countenance, we weaken
and succumb," the crowd

said staunchly. No room,
no table, no food,
but expectations:

"He gives us expectations,"
Sophie wept.
Like new plants and a trade

policy we can endorse:
tiny stars becoming galleons,
becoming moods.

Pentecost

The sun gone for a moment, air
intrudes itself, a cool presence, bodies
sit on the warm grass—

The word gone, the red letters
of speech—lips held open, tongue held still,
nothing but vowels, oh, ooh, the ah
of pain, the uh of hurt, the hhh of almost
nothing left, the hush of nothing except
the slightest breath—

                    the word gone, spirit
came, it filled, mouth to mouth,
the whole house.

            Then fire, a dazzle
of tongues, doing things over, things
that were done—

                the first breath breathed
        into something, then everyone
            talking at once—

A cloud slips from the shoulder
of the sun, the sun falls on the bodies stripped
again, the bodies houses filled with flesh—

For a moment, the house was nothing
but mouth, the tongue
of the body the tongue of the holiest ghost
of the word that was, that was to be—

Epiphany

At last, snow, flocked
like cotton, clusters, blossoms, stuff
comes down —

           so little wind you feel the pull,
as of apples, the weight of body
toward the knees —

        Hark! the Herald Angels Sing, bells
        announce, trumpets, wings, everything
        lifted, raised —

Down below, the grass is green, walks
are wet, people are carrying gloves
and bright umbrellas —

Not the flash, the blinding light, tongues,
as of fire, but the coming to see,
on the edge of a warm winter
like this,

        this shortened but lengthening day —

Coming to see, one feels less seen,
less haloed, held, more fallen
like snow turned rain
to earth to peace to mercy
to all that rages that aches that cries
that whimpers that turns that catches
its breath that breathes —

Resurrection

For Rose Marlovits Raden (1897–1978)

I

In my story the sisters forecast bad weather.
Twins born during the first harvest signal luck.

My great-grandmother and her sister are the magicians
of a town that never appears on a map of Hungary.

After her predictions of the peasant women's fertility,
after she warns of a drought that will burn the fields to dust,

after she's confessed the sins and graces of every citizen,
the priest holds the cup to my great-grandmother's lips

and the history of the women in this family unfolds —
scissors, table knives, razor blades skimming our wrists,

the wire to bite in the hospital driving lightning up
    the spine,
the solitude we refuse to call loneliness, the sickness

that rises again and again in our throats, the vinegar
to keep ourselves thin. My great-grandmother knows
    our story,

the story of the sisters who will follow her into the next
    world.

II

In Budapest, the traveling photographer mounts pictures
of dead children in albums, saving a lock of hair for
    each book.
Wearing dark dresses, matching handkerchiefs pressed
flat to the collarbone, the twins sit together, they wait.

When he holds the iron to their hair, steam rises over
their faces. The sisters hold still. Inside the frame
of the daguerreotype, pain isn't visible. No one in this city
knows the sisters. No one knows that one of us

will drink cologne in order to die. In the unnamed village
a coin with a double image still signifies luck.

III

In the New World, she beats the egg stiff for a strudel
and remembers synchronized steps across the potato fields,
arm in arm with her sister, their magic linked up.

In Europe angels guarded the beds of the dying.
The angels left my great-grandmother to cross
the ocean alone to her new life. The angels don't know

that I'll resurrect all the sisters. As the train
from Ellis Island drags along the horizon, the priest
lifts the bread and the wine to the mouths of the women

who ask for forgiveness, who plead for a safe, early death.

IV

Rose, when you come back to this world I'll be waiting,
suitcase at my side, with my camera, to follow you

to the next unnamed village, to find the last child
of the twentieth century, drowned in the well.

We rub matchsticks over her eyebrows. We paint
circles of rouge on her cheeks. We scorch each

of her curls with the iron. We fill her mouth with vinegar.
Together we prepare the girl for the Kingdom of Heaven.

In the country lit up by a powder flash of the camera,
the ashes that mark the sisters are blessed with the curse

you cast before you disappeared forever—your punishment,
Life Everlasting.

For Jude the Obscure

Sometimes I am brought so low
in my melancholy I know only you

can restore me: I turn to your book
in which Hardy has doomed you, line by line.

Taking you down, I have only to touch
the gold embossed title: now

my transport lifts me as if I had drunk
salvation's cup, eaten its bread.

Then, as I wander the day,
all I pass through are shadows

who would be my wife and children, students
I talk to, spectral, tenebrous,

so consumed was I with guilt
that I must devour you for myself,

take you in as a living sacrifice
who are not Christ but just a man

living only in small print
and then my memory. In his image Hardy made you

to set free someone you will never know
from the cage of himself that hunger

failing, to be for others
solace, respite, or a friend in need

himself of consolation, all of us
one beneath that wheel night and day

turning throughout the sky, imperceptible
pitiless, rolling over us.

Vespers

Now it is evening, the light rushes to fall
on a day disappearing into elemental shades,
the reddest red, blue's blue, the yellow yellowing going down.
Today is the first day of spring, lengthening
toward that ripening where it can start decline
from the long day in which I count each minute out
until dark falls and, exhausted, I am satisfied.

Mine is the world seen by Confucius, Jesus,
St. Teresa, by Dickinson, alone in her room,
facing a pit she opened on the floor, word by word,
granting her darkness as she spoke its resting place.
How can I dare to be afraid tonight,
part as I am of this earth turning to dust,
each breath propelling me by its eternity of motion?
How do I dare? Because I am nothing here,
light gone entirely now, like all of them,
like even one, without it gone.

Psalm before Sleep

Except for my body, who accompanies me
into this little death? Except for the stars
opening now on the vault overhead,

except for the barque I fit into so snugly,
my arms, my legs, shivering to dissolve,
dividing the great tides bearing me on.

Except for this song, the wind in my ears
which has joined the sky, reciting a black music
the constellations go on repeating in silence.

This is the way out: tomorrow I am someone else
I will meet face to face, the other shore arising.
This is the poem my words never bring back.

Radiance

Always that forgiving para-
noia. The Sisters of Charity
of the Incarnate Word, under
threats of violence, taking
down their art exhibit on sex
and AIDS, the sculptured geni-
talia, the angel fucking at
the altar. Neither Lucifer,
nor Gabriel. One of a lesser
order. In radiance, even so.
All slow. Unhurried. No
rush to revelation. Just
the wind along your arm. Or
flat-bottomed, noble clouds
boating a clear, summer sky.
Or the name of some place
local and familiar. So it
begins (doesn't it?). God
appearing to Saint Francis,
Saint Ludmila, Saint Ansgar—
as flocks of birds, a loaf
of bread, a man with hounds
and shotgun. God in the gar-
bage, in the stares of children,
the mouths of charlatans.
Oak, shagbark hickory, beech.
When what I need's the soul
of a breath of wisdom I don't
have, sitting here at evening
under the trees, empty rose-
light lighter than any thought
of it, caught in the tangled
tracery of ordinary branches.

A Capella

I'm standing here in the church
of oaks and hickories, in the chapel
of winter mulberries and leafless
cherries. In the church of the long,
dry creek akindle with moonlight
on snowmelt. I'm standing here under
Mercury and Venus, under Cepheus
and Cassiopeia, under the dark vault
of the dragon and the bear, getting
cold in this cold cathedral of stars,
warming my blood with whiskey, my
hands in a little chapel of smoke.
I'm standing at the shrine of Our
Lady of the Sunday night steak
and the broiled potato, the Virgin
of mixed greens and crusted bread.
Tart saint of Chardonnays and tall
Bordeaux and peppery Burgundy.
I'm standing here thinking about
the perfect emptiness of it;
of the warmth that will touch me
when I open the door and see you
at dinner by firelight in this
house we built with our own hands.

Pietà

A mother and her son tug
up out of a dumpster
a mirror, body-
length, un-
broken.

Bowing, he thrusts his closed eyes into his mom's floral
blouse.
He sniffs the gardenia-scented shampoo in the gray curls of
her hair;
he adores their sweet fragility, so soft against his cheek.

On a peach-colored late spring afternoon,
in his queen-sized bed, he bent
into a question mark, and beat off,
for the first time, his attacker,
planting, in his navel, the seeds
of a sex addict's future, banging

on the locked green door of the condemned bath house,
weeping as the bus split, minus one, for the orgy,
him hunched over a porn periodical, feeling
some hot stranger's glance pass
over him,

away,
the dark night of his dong a summer day.

Mother, may one
come inside the air, its butterflies
fluttering around a hummingbird?

Coyotes whine, their voices
infantile, effeminate, like
the cries of mothers and their babies
shoved, for Heaven's sake, into the ovens.

God's Cut-Off TV Screen's Vanishing Mirror Seems an Unshared Point

1.

Unlike talk, like prayer, this mist unravels
skeins of sweat across the lake's green skin,
censoring, then exposing, lanky scrub pines
quivering against white blossoms of dogwood
inverted deep inside Earth's paperthin mirror.

Is this some form of prank, or prayer,
this squirrel skeleton hanged overhead,
crucified upon a black telephone cable,
the twiglike arms hooked over that vine
our masks chitchat through silently?

Skull a blown-out walnut, socket-
holes bored for this giant rosary,
a conversation piece of deaths, see,
savior, my blackened delicacy grilled
under your stare, your high-noon fire.

2.

One spring night, I trembled frozen, caught
against white rapids in the eyes of a bone face,
an East Indian cab driver witnessing
at me more than an hour, ignoring
his idling livelihood behind him.

Smile against my face, he whispered,
Listen. When they reel Him down,
His visage all twisted in agony,
His fluorescent orbs exploding, moving
across each bearer's mask, down

to one's own quivering
lips, it's love, not death,
feeds us His burning
prayer to flesh,
this mortal form.

The Soul as a Body

There's a body inside the body.
It's the form that rises up, immune
to fire. It's the kingdom of nothing
as a body. High nothing! You see
its shell in the mirror, draw back.
Feel ashamed. It wakes in a dream
and speaks in silence. Suffers names.
What do you call it? The one as two?
Grain of salt? Eater of seeds?
Behold its raiment as it transfigures.
A threadless garment-force as form.
Fatal shroud. You cannot touch it.
It rises from your groin like a quail
with vertical power. Leaps like a trout
to catch the fly in an arc that spans
the world. There is a medium inside
the body like water or air in which
this other body swims and flies, is quick
to disappear, you, yet not you. Each being
a surprise of need's design. Each need
determined by another need until
there's only beauty. The more you dress
it up in a single form the less you see
what you cannot see at first. The less
you know the multitudes contained inside you.
It is a body that has come to you
with a passionate love. That sees itself
in all things. That cannot live without you.

Because You Mentioned the Spiritual Life

A lone tern turns in the blowsy wind,
and there's the ocean and its timbrous repetitions,
and what a small pleasure it is
that the shade, halfway down,
poorly conceals the lovers next door.
    Fishing boats and sea air,
the moon now on the other side of our world
influencing happiness and crime.
The spiritual life, I'm thinking, is worthless
unless it's another way of having a good time.
    To you I'll say it's some quiet gaiety
after a passage through what's difficult,
perhaps dangerous. I'd like to please you.
So many travelers going to such a small state—
I can see the ferry, triple-tiered and white,
on its way to Delaware.
    I'm peeling and sectioning
an orange. I'm slipping a section into my mouth.
What a perfect thing an orange is
to think about.
    I should say to you
the spiritual life is what cannot be had
through obeisance, but we'll get nowhere
with talk like this.
A darning needle just zoomed by.
The dune grass is leaning west.
    Come join me on the deck,
the gulls are squawking, and an airplane
pulling a banner telling us where to eat
is flying low over the sand castles
and body sculptures the children have built.
The tide will have them soon. Moments
are what we have.

Religion

First, it was more about mystery than about trying to get us to
behave. Whichever, we're still in some lonely cave, not far from
that moment a lightning storm or a sunset drove us to invent the
upper reaches of the sky. Religion is proof that a good story,
well-told, is a powerful thing. Proof, too, that terror makes
fabulists of us all. We're pitiful, finally, and so oddly valiant. The
dead god rising into ism after ism — that longing for coherence
that keeps us, if not naive, historically challenged. To love Christ
you must love the Buddha, to love Mohammed or Moses you
must love Confucius and, say, Schopenhauer and Nietzsche as
well. They were all wise and unsponsored and insufficient, some
of the best of us. I'm saying this to myself: the sacred cannot be
found unless you give up some old version of it. And when you
do, mon semblable, mon frère, I swear there'll be an emptiness
it'll take a lifetime to fill. Indulge, become capacious, give up
nothing, Jack my corner grocer said. He was pushing the
portobellos, but I was listening with that other, my neediest ear.

The Shiny Aluminum of God

Carolina, Puerto Rico, 1997

After the pilgrimage
to the Office of Cemetery Records,
we pay fifty dollars in cash
for the free municipal burial plot,
the clerk hiding the bills in a manila folder.
El pastor Pentecostal forgets the name of the dead,
points at the ceiling and gazes up
whenever he loudly whispers the syllables
for eternal life, *la vida eterna,*
as if the stain on the tile were the map of heaven.
The mourners are palm trees in the hallelujah wind,
hands raised overhead. Once grandmother Tata's pen
looped the words of the spirits as they spoke to her;
now she grips a borrowed golden crucifix
in the coffin, lid propped open by mistake.
The coffin bumps into a hole of mud
next to the chain-link fence, and then
the family Vélez Espada gathers for dinner.

The pernil is frozen, pork shoulder congealed and raw
like a hunk of Siberian woolly mammoth.
But Angela tells us of the miracle pot
that will roast the meat in an hour
without a cup of water. She sells the pot
to her neighbors too, keeps a tower of boxes
with a picture of the pot resplendent on every box.
The words on her kerchief hail
the shiny aluminum of God: Dios te ama.

The scar carves her husband's forehead
where the doctors scooped the tumor out,
where cancer cells scramble like a fistful of ants.
In a year he will be the next funeral, when the saints

of oncology surrender their weapons. For now
Edwin lives by the finches he snares in the backyard,
wings blundering through the trapdoor of the cage,
sold for five dollars apiece to the neighbors.
He praises God for brain surgery and finches,
leans close and grins about the time
his brother somersaulted out a window
and two swooping angels caught him
by the elbows, inches from the ground.
Only one broken rib, Edwin says,
rubbing his stomach in the slow way
of a man satisfied with his meal.
Angela's brother passes out pamphlets:
God's ambulance found him and his needle
in a condemned building, no shoes
and no heartbeat. Then Edwin says:
God will not let me die.

An hour later,
the pernil is still frozen in the oven.
Angela stares at the sweating pork,
then the boxes of pots unsold in the corner.
A boy cousin taps his fork
and asks if we can eat the finches.
The trap clatters in the backyard,
an angel flapping in the cage.

Tantum Ergo

What here redeems us? Surely
not this posture of reverence
before the tabernacle's hasp

pinned into place, nor that
tiny burnished door, secure
beneath a candle flame. The cosmic

burst when finally it hinges
open—the host removed—
leaves the all-too-ponderable

space: another empty tomb.
And now the monstrance,
blinding almost beyond reason,

voices acceding to Aquinas's
hymn, amid heady swirls
of frankincense and organ swell,

the aggrieved bones' reverberations;
each sense amening even
to the brink—but then this

undersong throbbing through
the temples, its insistent
Miserere lapping like the tide.

Petit Mal

This is how, perhaps,
we first came to know
the gods: tiny ailment,

a sudden advent of dread,
and more dread in the shuddering
wake: how the mind hinged

open to the unforeseen
dimension, the chaotic prime,
stirred brew of all

we ever were: we
could not live there, could
not bear to have the world's

remnants we had stitched
into a coat of lights
ripped, then remade again

and again: yet here's this
swaddling aura, this nimbus
we're stunned each time to wear.

The Life Everlasting

At the foot of the wall
dark-robed crickets end their singing
in the brittle grass.

But above, long rows of windows
funnel sunlight in, and inside,
two trapped wasps stagger

doubly stunned against the glass:
unexpected warmth in December kindles
the flame-yellow, ash-black bellies.

Dully awake, throbbing like larvae
again, they crawl from a crevice
into this room, to strike

and spin and fall, obsessed and
helpless. Is it only their desire
to go back over their lives

that sends them repeatedly
up this impossible trek?
Or is it that the air in here

is too sweet, too warm
and they want the ice and shadow
that would end the farce?

It is fifteen years since I used
to slip out early to hide in the car,
wanting to leap at the glass—

to break through to anything else—
when the pent-up heat of noon,
fading chords and choruses,

and cloying perfumes
sickened me after the Methodists'
Easter services.

Cash or Turtle or Heaven

Just beyond that big sign for Ebenezer Church?—
you know the one—and Ellsworth's Polled Herefords?—
I had to swerve to miss a turtle in the lane
and I looked in the rearview and I saw the pickup
behind me, that was loaded too high anyway
with old furniture and all, swerve in order to
hit the damn thing, and I hope it set
the sonofabitch back about five lifetimes.
Lindy sitting next to me, all she could
talk about was getting new sunglasses, like mine,
said she wanted the Zodiac ones, though,
so she could personally express herself, *her* sign.
What about you? Do any camping? Like to fish?
I just can't get away much these days, I'm short of cash.

* * * *

The boss knows what's best for you, you don't
have to ask him for anything, he already
knows what you need, so every morning you should
hunch over your coffee and say this prayer:
Our father, which art
in business, incorporated be thy name.
Thy profit come, thy will be done,
at work as it is in Congress.
Give us this day our daily wage.
And extend our credit, as we have had
to give you those benefit concessions.
And lead us not into grievances or strikes,
but deliver us from unions: for thine
is the profit, and the power, and the lobby forever. Amen.

* * * *

But I never will have all the cash I need.
That's a hell of a thing, that turtle, isn't it?

I hit a goddamn deer once, it broke
the windshield and smashed the fender in
like it was tinfoil—surprise you—I had it made
into sausage, though, and we ate that
for a whole winter. That was even before
I lost my job. Could use the meat now,
even getting it that way. And before Lindy
started going back to church with the kids.
I don't like to go much, I wasn't raised to it
like she was, don't see the point. If there is
a heaven, they got to keep some of these
goddamned bastards out of there, I say and believe.

Pentecost

Neither the sorrows of afternoon, waiting in the silent
    house,
Nor the night no sleep relieves, when memory
Repeats its prosecution.

Nor the morning's ache for dream's illusion, nor any
    prayers
Improvised to an unknowable god
Can extinguish the flame.

We are not as we were. Death has been our pentecost,
And our innocence consumed by these implacable
Tongues of fire.

Comfort me with stones. Quench my thirst with sand.
I offer you this scarred and guilty hand
Until others mix our ashes.

The Litany

This is a litany of lost things,
a canon of possessions dispossessed,
a photograph, an old address, a key.
It is a list of words to memorize
or to forget—of *amo, amas, amat,*
the conjugations of a dead tongue
in which the final sentence has been spoken.

This is the liturgy of rain,
falling on mountain, field, and ocean—
indifferent, anonymous, complete—
of water infinitesimally slow,
sifting through rock, pooling in darkness,
gathering in springs, then rising without our agency,
only to dissolve in mist or cloud or dew.

This is a prayer to unbelief,
to candles guttering and darkness undivided,
to incense drifting into emptiness.
It is the smile of a stone madonna
and the silent fury of the consecrated wine,
a benediction on the death of a young god,
brave and beautiful, rotting on a tree.

This is a litany to earth and ashes,
to the dust of roads and vacant rooms,
to the fine silt circling in a shaft of sun,
settling indifferently on books and beds.
This is a prayer to praise what we become,
"Dust thou art, to dust thou shalt return."
Savor its taste—the bitterness of earth and ashes.

This is a prayer, inchoate and unfinished,
for you, my love, my loss, my lesion,
a rosary of words to count out time's

illusions, all the minutes, hours, days
the calendar compounds as if the past
existed somewhere—like an inheritance
still waiting to be claimed.

Until at last it is our litany, *mon vieux*,
my reader, my voyeur, as if the mist
steaming from the gorge, this pure paradox,
the shattered river rising as it falls—
splintering the light, swirling it skyward,
neither transparent nor opaque but luminous,
even as it vanishes—were not our life.

from Holiday

X
October 1
(morning)

Mother, two days ago he left
with another woman
for a tour of Jerusalem.
Together they'll visit the Old City,
including Mount Zion and the tunnel
excavations under the Wall; arrive
at the Jewish Quarter and the Citadel Museum;
walk along the Cardo, the underground
Roman Street; be driven to the Masada
and ascend the rock fortress where the Zealots
made their last stand, then took their own
lives. *He is not a Zealot, but I
believe in suicide.* Then, they'll swim in the Dead

Sea and enjoy the mud
baths. *It rained here yesterday
on your grave and the grass over
it was so sparse and soft—the ground
a sponge. If I would have chosen, could I have dug
down to you?* Tomorrow or the day after

they go to Mount Nebo, the burial place
of Moses. *How many Commandments
can anyone handle?* Will he think of you
before *that* grave? Those long months
of your dying, when he'd disappear—
was it to be with her? And when he visits

the "rose red city" of Petra—carved
out of solid rock, surrounded by soaring
temples and elaborate tombs—will he

(57

think of the empty red suit that your bones are dressed in?
The healthy fleece covered by an oily
substance that protects the sheep
from the rain, forever dried out.

(afternoon)

I wished him a good trip—was polite—
and can only imagine
what it would be like to be at
Vad Va'Shem—the memorial to the six million—
and what the synagogue with the Chagall stained
windows might look like when the sun hits
the glass at high noon. *Here, the sun hit
your plaque, creating a wet, golden maple leaf
effect that you would have liked.
Your favorite season has arrived
without you* and he's gone

to Old Jaffa, Tel Aviv, the Diaspora
Museum. Soon, we'll all be scattered
relics beneath the ground, waiting only
for some archaeologist to dig up
and examine. *Let him go,
I said to my hand, my closed palm.
His last trip to the holy
land, that's what he said.* A place
I've never been and probably never
will be, my eyes just left to absorb the *angered*

red I see over
and over. Is that the reason—your fury
over dying, *over him*—why you insisted
on a suit of rage, slowly becoming invisible,
outside the spectrum of what we could possibly see?

(night)

My brain can no longer organize
the nerve signals and my green thoughts

are a jumble—
hardly the complement to what
you are shredded in.
I have stumbled through the spectrum
of emotion—gone full circle
on the wheel, spun
from yellow to orange to purple,
have ground through all the blues
and always come back
from my inward travels to you—
undone by what is done—
to leave only the sun-
flowers on your autumn grave—forever
the honeybee hovering near home
for any hope of pollen.

The Arch of Sanctification

The Arch of Sanctification, St. Louis
Cathedral, depicts the Holy Spirit
as a dove in God's chest.

I could use a dove in my heart.
I could use this God of Italian tile,
Lee Marvin in dreadlocks, light surging
from head and hands, Zeus-circuitry
spewing gold and only slightly
less prophetic than St. Louis sun.
Go now, His heart says, and be plain
all your years: Scheherazade awaits.
Go now and live mute among lepers:
their suffering is also song.
Go now and kiss your enemies
hard at the lips like the clasp
of revelation: the taste of malice
is also sacred. You, Holy Spirit,
were the one I never got, a pixie,
to wound the Catholic lexicon,
though without pranks, Trinity's wisp,
carrier of sanctification. Meaning what?
This is the fog the Sisters offered: walls
must be led to faith, stones softened
to belief. This the confounding sincerity
of the Priest: through the Spirit
our poor bones were created. I lower mine
into the creaking music of a pew.
I could use a dove in my heart
because wanting's made it small, no room
for wings or a civil wish. Even now
I want this mosaic, to carry
and adore it to pieces, down to sketch,
down to the artist's hands mapping the tiles,
sweating until he hears the voice of God

and why not. I hear the voice of God
all the time, god of an agnostic, a whisper
that says you must love better, must love
more. I devise the moment's theology:
Spirit's the comfort of vanishing
into the palm of a cathedral
where I'm mixed, part and parcel,
woven back into the father and son,
the word of myself. In an hour
I'll come apart in a hotel room,
bad habits and ice, one window and finally
me in a chair staring at the red lights
of an antenna, writing the list
of whose fault this is. Against that time
I memorize the sweep of wings, let
white feathers stain my eyes.
Saints in designer robes look down,
thin as Byzantium. If I pray
it's to taunt, to beg them to speak.

Between Worlds

So many mornings I awoke
to the impatient chant of
a faithful man, phylactery
strapped to his forehead and forearm,
a chapped leather book in
the prayer of his hands, and
weaving back and forth as if
tugged by an invisible rope,
an umbilical force, something
behind and beyond him.
How strange it was and still is
to see someone you know and love,
someone easy and quick with
a bad joke and a hard laugh,
in the service of their god.
The room would be blue with
the day's new beginnings or
dark in its threshold, and the street
was always busy with the clamor
of tired, complaining neighbors
who either hated their jobs
or loved them.
It was the real world,
the world outside that room,
the world that I lived in and
like everyone else, would never
understand.
How I watched this man,
each and every morning, who
in the firm moments of his broochas
was not so much my grandfather
as someone wondrously anonymous,
someone who excited me
by engaging something solemn,
something powerful, something I would

never find devotion for.
There were so many questions,
so many secrets, so many things
that could never be learned, and not
even in those mornings did I once
believe he brought both worlds
any closer together.
And then years later, when I,
dressed in a silk talis, weaving
and bowing, and weeping in Kaddish
for him, when I mourned the loss
of a man who died contented,
I felt that vicarious power,
that gave license to my doubt,
that troubled me to no end,
that conducted the untold secrets
between one world and another,
and I knew it was important,
and I knew it was impossible.

American Heaven

As the century
winds up shopping
in a suburban

mall transcendent as
neon, debris of
all that's known

is massive as
the evening. Wax
statues of Elvis

and Jesus. Laughter
in an orchard.
Genuine animal sadness.

Shining like icons,
electrocuted fish float
beneath a bridge

then sink as
we expected through
our very senses.

The world is
smeared with this
until the fog

drifts in, erasing
shapes and forms
like clintonia's pink

in dazzling aftermaths
breaking light in
canyons as summer

thickens burls above
the witch's butter
on golden slime

mold trails where
fire once burned
inside a tree

that grows around
that scar. We
can stand there

now within a
spray of sun.
Flamingos in the

wild against the
falsest dawn are
present as a

sign. A tapestry
of sensations painted
on the brain.

The blue scent
of mirrors the
speeding world resembles.

Hell

If you want to understand the social and political
history of modern man, study hell.

—THOMAS MERTON

It's probably like the excitement of your first cigarette, but it lasts
forever, that dizzying nausea—the Unknown: sulphuric clouds,
infernal helpers scurrying around with imitation human heads
on their buttocks, bats leaping from black books, dragon tails
waving, monkey glands everywhere, hope dying slowly like a bad
marriage, "I am nobody" the only conversation.

But then again the damned might be as recognizable and
stupid as the living: men who use the same condom twice,
women who let them, the degenerate who molested Spider-
Man—everyone perpetually suing each other, holding hands in a
circle whose rim clangs like a counterfeit coin.

But more likely it's the general humiliation of being dead,
realizing your own personal Beelzebub might be the least weird
guy you know.

Enigma of the Stigma, or Vice Versa

(For Genevieve)

I'm drawn to the ineffable, yet cathedrals leave me empty, the charismatic next door has no imagination, near misses of comets go unexplained by theories of emanation—all frauds, unsoiled neck braces piled in empty corners.

But I trust the stem of this feather, its eye a spot on the pillow where she lays her head, her rump warming the hollow of my stomach, lilies sprouting from a book on her nightstand, a perfumed hair creasing my tongue. . . . Mysteries inviting both penetration and erasure.

Genesis: A Retrospective

It began with division. He knows this. He can read: "God was pleased with the light that He saw, and He *separated* the light from the darkness. God called the light Day, and He called the darkness Night. Thus evening came, and morning—first day." Italics, His? He couldn't be sure after so many years. Maybe He was in transition, or just made weary by His creations—or perhaps "divisions" was the right word. All He remembered were cramps in His legs and arms, His head hurting from so many possibilities.

Change a few words here and there, that's all He had to do.

But there'd always be incarnations, innuendos.

Five from Three

Reach

When we heard the tree hum,
I was far beyond words, so far
inside the world I was only atoms—
a song singing to itself, inside the wind
of matter. When all the shrubs and
grasses splayed themselves to catch
the warmth from interstellar space,
my hands were vegetation too,
sunstruck, like every being. And so
was my desire, my reach towards you,

my wish to speak a language
of high flung music and earthliness.

Coast

I thought I found the answer when
the blackbirds formed a swarm,
hovered, lofted off at high speed,
veered, became a composition
of light-dark motion; sometimes ten
or twenty flew apart, a counterpoint, then
re-collided with the main-flock, merged
into one impulse—one mind among
a hundred soaring bodies, played
in twilight, brought night down
onto us, out of pink and blue:

so elated, darkness hardly mattered.

Tap

I love to find a door. Like the spinal tap—
above the draped fetal curve, you work
the trocar inwards. Dowser, boatman,

auger, bore. Every surface has its opening,
even bone. Steel finds fossa, penetrates.
That give, as the needle enters dura.
Slide out the central metal filament,
it rings, and the invisible emerges, drop
by drop, caught in transparent tubes. So

much fineness—glass and silver, the white
field, crystalline fluid. Seek and you find.
How it comes, the brain's clear bath.

Light

The morning when I first notice
the leaves starting to color,
early orange, and back-lit,
I think how rapture doesn't
vanish, merely fades into
the background, waits for those
moments between moments.

I think this and the door opens,
the street takes on its glistening
look, Bay fog lifting, patches of sun
on sycamore—yellow sea.
I am in again, and swimming.

The World

My ears echo too loudly,
everything too much, turtle,
without my shell. I am a gong
that has been unstruck.
Still reverberating from
what is taken away, and
never was. A thousand sharp
leaves press against the window,
that tide, the clank of my spoon
against the blue china mug,

it doesn't take much
to make music.

You Keep Coming upon Your Breath at the Altar

Has he walked away from the temple? Has he taken
your shoes? Your socks with those red sandstone stains?

Durga Temple had been hot yesterday, the floor wet from
the hose. Thousands of prayers clung to you as you walked.

Today at the Ananda Moyi Ma Temple, you try to lose
your breath to the cooling swell of incense.

How many died during the Indian Mutiny, you're not sure.
Were British bullets really greased with pig fat? With cow fat?

And how might one know if a touch is real,
or just flesh? Moist, or simply tongue?

You keep coming upon your breath at the altar, imagine
walking home barefoot through alleys of broken glass.

A rumor may kill. A remote goat bell on the steps
of the ghat somehow sounds like thunder off the river.

Cremation ash drifts by like wedges of night.
Tiny bats dropping into the Ganges current.

Takahashi Shinkichi said, *The sparrow is the mightiest
    creature
in the world*, but you're certain he was never in Benares
    in May.

You keep coming back to breath, restlessly stirring
thoughts, coming upon an altar and a sleeping snake.

If the breath would calm, the snake might lift its great golden
head for you to polish. Might open its mouth, unwind its tail.

The mosquito net over your bed somehow comes untucked
in the middle of each night. Death becomes almost holy.

It is talked about in the streets, whispered on corners as
eel-fire, given as diksha in the ashram, as sex on the cot.

Even eaten as over-spiced dal. It is rubbed with rags,
with cigarette butts. With turmeric and broiled beets.

In Bombay, your friends could not control the rubbing,
said that, *Getting malaria would one day be our fate.*

See: the paper tallies floods and tells you how to die.
The astrologer finds milk, even in the testicles of Taurus.

Now the temple priest brings prasad, sanctified sweets.
Hundreds of ants as thin brown veins in the little balls.

You keep coming upon tiny electrical currents
zigzagging lightning on the altar of the spine.

You keep coming upon breath like the flit of a sparrow
bringing you bone bruise as song.

You open your eyes, see the mat outside, the old man,
your shoes, a singeing bat. Even food at your feet.

Baksheesh for the old man guarding my shoes, you think.
Two rupees should be enough to tell you you're still alive.

The Lamps Are Brought In

Mother Kali, the destroyer, is the giver
of all life. Then the doors in the spine open

and the lamps are brought in. The allergist
gives himself an injection of eel grass

and tree pollen, foams at the mouth, wonders
if the bumps on his skin are real

or imagined. The motorcycle parked
by the peepal tree draws more flies

than the water-buffalo on campus bathing in monsoon
mud. Can you feel heat lightning in your palm

as you enter the library and gnaw on a rubber hose?
Slap it across the back of a braying

donkey who chews prayer beads in the back
of a Tantric text? As you touch the uncurved

leather, longing for it to be round and bruised
with spokes? As you paint the wall of your puja room

with the ocher robes of a Hindu holy man and have visions
of an ancient fertility cult passing a goldfish

around a fire, chanting your name
centuries before your birth? Can you hear

molecules of struggle in a tuba tossed in a rut
to rust in the pen of some Benares pig farm?

You can trade malaria pills on the black market
for vegetable pakora, careful

to have the skins boiled and peeled?
Under Kali's feet, Lord Shiva's prostrate body,

though appearing dead, is not dead.
His erect penis beneath the curve

of her full blue thighs is the giver
of all life. Then the doors in the spine open

and you hear the bleeding of crickets
in your groin. Threads of running water. A faucet

that drops filaments of the Milky Way
down through your medulla

into your scrotum. A piece of rope burns
like a piranha in southern summer shoals.

Gold carp, gold carp, gold carp, the rishi
chants in Sanskrit, drawing your outline in the mud.

The hanged man is a peyote blossom on the tip
of a cactus. No, the hanged man has an erection,

then an ejaculation at the precise moment
of death. He sways from a peepal tree

on India's northern plain like a bloated prayer flag
or a massive bag of feed before all who pass.

Like a moment of table salt you might think
twice about before seasoning the lamb.

Banaras Is Another Name for the World

A sadhu carries a lamp to the Ganges,
unwinds his long hair into the river.

The Milky Way glitters in mud, twigs,
snags of carp, and ashes of millions.

Were they content over the evening dal?
Did they like tea? How were they touched?

Banaras is another name for the world.
Ganga, for the mother of the world.

You count the goats on the steps
of the bathing ghat and consider a new profession.

Maybe the chai wallah understands
the goats better than the goatherd?

New constellations form in the pail. Sagittarius
is not a mineral deficiency detailed in stools.

Whenever opposites attract, cobblestones shift a little and
the street curves inward at an almost undetectable slope.

You wander old Muslim neighborhoods on Madanpura on your
way to Chowk, sense the love of God even in cooking meat.

See how smoke from cremation grounds speckles the river?
You want to step in but you've seen the dead cow.

You've seen the purple corpse when you took the boat.
You've seen the men urinating against the wall.

Where is the gold carp and where is your foot?
How might you bathe in the river without getting in?

Exodus

Pillar of cloud by day,
Pillar of fire by night.

Moses, your false beard was burning.
An undomesticated guise, don't you think?

Slaughtering all the firstborn in Egypt.
Teaching livestock the Ten Commandments.

If locusts drive the pharaoh into despair,
The slaves will never learn to suffer.

If the slaves never learn to suffer,
Then let's forget the pyramids altogether.

For argument's sake, let's just say the pyramids were
    put here
By life forms from Planet of the Damned.

I saw them in my favorite nightmare,
The one where they amend the little girl's skin

With a blowtorch. Yes, I could spend my whole life
Watching a moth destroy itself against a light bulb.

But I could never imagine that light bulb
As anything more than my powerless life.

Pillar of cloud by day,
Pillar of fire by night.

God Lovingly Counterattacks

Happy-go-lucky and lazy. We took things
As they came.

Our town paid dearly for it.

Who lit these fat candles? Whiter than the milky bones
Of a damaged angel. Look how they flicker
In the heart's wreckage.

Jaws of Life snapped shut on your supermodel's face.

Wooden floors impregnated with oil from the machinery. Wool fluff
Forming sticky deposits against the walls. Factory becomes
A blazing cathedral. Someone tries to put out the flames
By beating them with his cap. When this fails,
We descend the ladder. Down to the Zero.
Now here we are listening to the erratic
Heartbeat of God. Barefoot
In our black veils. Drunk
In our unbearable
Wedding gowns.
Our souls?

      Scraped clean.

Dixit Insipiens

At first, it was only a trickle
Of eminent men, with their astrolabes and armillae,
Who passed cautious notes to each other, obscurely worded.
Of course the terrible news leaked out
And the peasants were agitated.
Moans arose from the windowless hovels.
Men, hardly human, shouldering crude farm implements,
Gathered in knots along the roads and raved:
Storm the great houses! Smash the laboratory,
The retorts, the lenses—instruments of Satan.
But the minions of the manors
Lashed them back from the bronze gates,
Back to the foetid darkness, where they scoured their knees,
Praying for us.

The magnificent correspondence between Madame A.
And the more eminent, though less notorious,
Monsieur B. reveals a breathtaking indifference
To you: not even the target of a bilious epigram.
They move intently toward their prime concern:
Which voice, this time, will loose
Its thunderbolt? The straggling troops of revolution
Must be rallied yet again.
In perfect confidence of their powers,
As if they, who after all are people of flesh and bone,
Despite their attainments, had replaced you;
Not by storming the throne-room, nor by those manifestos
They so supremely compose.
You were swept out, and they swept in, that's all.

Out there, on the edge of the familiar world,
Are knots of men, burned dark as our own peasants
Used to be, but better armed, we know;
We armed them.
From time to time they bang their heads on the sand

And shout, unintelligibly, of you.
Their version of you, of course, quite different
From the blandness you metamorphosed into
Over the centuries, progressively edited.
Holy war! Can they be in earnest?
After all, this isn't the fourteenth century.
Is it the uneasiness we feel, or the remnants
Of ancestral superstition, which makes us ask ourselves,
Can this be your planned revenge?

How can you be vengeful when you don't exist?
If only the weight of centuries
Wasn't on your side.
If only unbelief was more like faith.

Jack in the Box

Jack at Jack in the Box
is not at table or counter;
he is in the box, of course.

I see myself in a box,
    but not with him.
Kafka's coffee in it
dreams of an island.
Swallowing the steam,
    I am a box now.

Behind the wall is
Mail Boxes Etc.
All are the boxes, etc., etc.
and the I, etc. in the box.

Still dark when we file like children out on the turf,

Yet our hymn is *For the Beauty of the Earth.*
Irony scourges. Is that how grown-ups atone?
The apostate, Jack, is back with us. It's cancer.

We've gathered, we few others, by the river
For other reasons, whatever. Where's the sun?
Sunrise Service. Easter. Ice on the waters.

In the flow, among black limbs, a jug bobs past us,
Empty, thrown perhaps by a drunken angler
Who waited through last fall but never caught him,

The fish he'd prayed for, childlike—unseeable, awesome.
We here know life is hard but for some promise.
We murmur *For the Love which from our birth. . . .*

Debris, relentless, eddies down from north.
I imagine the fisherman, grown more doubtful
    than Thomas:
One dusk he flung away the jug, the dream.

Is that a Christmas present, still in its carton?
Over and around us lies, we sing.
We have mouthed the store-bought dough, the bitter wine.

They are real enough, the wounds we've seen.
Last Wednesday, shocked, we buried redoubtable Vernon.
We'd all feel different, maybe, in different weather.

It would seem somehow less *willed,* this banding together.
We have left undone the things we ought to have done,
And the other way round. Jane's at the clinic. Neurosis.

Harley's halt again. Accursed phlebitis.
Flotsam—fragmented story—drifts and spins.
What was it that the Samaritan woman said?

A man who told me all I ever did.
The pastor opened by reading about her from John.
Lazarus too. And the blind man's pool at Silóam.

As a fish-eye sun slides open over the mountain,
Our children strain to break from us and play.
We end with *This our hymn of grateful praise.*

—John 4:29;

—⸺ 20:25;

—⸺ 11;

—⸺ 9

Do not trust in these deceptive words:

This is the temple of the Lord,
The temple of the Lord. . . .
First Lenten Sunday, and the Jeremiad

Reduces us to heretics,
Quite properly: the temple draws us inward
Yet again. "Quebec Express"

—The wind along our glacial reach of river—
Penetrates through nailholes, sockets.
The fellowship, however, gathers.

Till service starts, we throw clichés at winter,
Chatting to unlock it,
Warm ourselves. The litany assures,

Its scope so narrow:
Oh yes, we say and pray, they'll all be here:
Jonquils; jobs; the chanting thrush; the sparrow. . . .

Blooms and babies, issues of the town.
How spring will nap the lawns.
Someone's good news to celebrate—

Remission. Calm. Some novel revenue
To keep the school afloat:
"Revenue," says Blaise: "The coming back."

It's not such puns nor platitudes that soothe
But how they do come back.
Not peace, we're warned. *A sword.*

Not, thus, to trust in children, flowers, birds?
Nor mist all raiment-soft on open water?
And not these words, nor pungency of lumber

That fell, before last fall, before the blade?
It isn't them we trust in any case
But their return, as sure as ours.

The season's myth declines to death,
And yet again, again, we park our cars
And move inside to speak our faith.

                                    —Jeremiah 7:4;
                                    —Matthew 10:34

A Table in the Wilderness

I draw a window
and a man sitting inside it.

I draw a bird in flight above the lintel.

That's my picture of *thinking*.

If I put a woman there instead
of the man, it's a picture of *speaking*.

If I draw a second bird
in the woman's lap, it's *ministering*.

A third flying below her feet.
Now it's *singing*.

Or erase the birds,
make ivy branching
around the woman's ankles, clinging
to her knees, and it becomes *remembering*.

You'll have to find your own
pictures, whoever you are,
whatever your need.

As for me, many small hands
issuing from a waterfall
means silence
mothered me.

The hours hung like fruit in night's tree
means when I close my eyes
and look inside me,

a thousand open eyes
span the moment of my waking.

(85

Meanwhile, the clock
adding a grain to a grain
and not getting bigger,

subtracting a day from a day
and never having less, means the honey

lies awake all night
inside the honeycomb
wondering who its parents are.

And even my death isn't my death
unless it's the unfathomed brow
of a nameless face.

Even my name isn't my name
except the bees assemble

a table to grant a stranger
light and moment in a wilderness
of *Who? Where?*

Nativity

In the dark, a child might ask, *What is the world?*
just to hear his sister
promise, *An unfinished wing of heaven,*
just to hear his brother say,
A house inside a house,
but most of all to hear his mother answer,
One more song, then you go to sleep.

How could anyone in that bed guess
the question finds its beginning
in the answer long growing
inside the one who asked, that restless boy,
the night's darling?

Later, a man lying awake,
he might ask it again,
just to hear the silence
charge him, *This night
arching over your sleepless wondering,*

*this night, the near ground
every reaching-out-to overreaches,*

just to remind himself
out of what little earth and duration,
out of what immense good-bye,

each must make a safe place of his heart,
before so strange and wild a guest
as God approaches.

Little Round

My fool asks: Do the years spell a path to later
be remembered? Who's there to read them back?

My death says: One bird knows the hour and suffers
to house its millstone-weight as song.

My night watchman lies down
in a room by the sea
and hears the water telling,
out of a thousand mouths,
the story behind his mother's sleeping face.

My eternity shrugs and yawns:
Let the stars knit and fold
inside their numbered rooms. When night asks
who I am I answer, *Your own*, and am not lonely.

My loneliness, my sleepless darling
reminds herself
the fruit that falls increases
at the speed of the body rising to meet it.

And my child? He sleeps and sleeps.

And my mother? She divides
the rice, today's portion from tomorrow's,
tomorrow's from ever after.

And my father. He faces me and rows
toward what he can't see.

And my God.
What have I done with my God?

Anthills

It's true that my soul   mea culpa   is empty
but maybe it's supposed to be empty   Maybe
it's more like a monk's cell than a Victorian
living room   In the darkness I scratch a line on
my soul's bare wall   meaning One more day   scratch the son
of a bitch *off*   So that's what life means: *One more day*
Not very enlightening   but what am I   a

Roman candle   like Virgil singing "Arms and the
Man"?   My grandma crocheted doilies that were always
floating off the arms of our overstuffed chairs and
sofas like huge soiled snowflakes   *To pass the day* she
said   I'm more like Grandma than Virgil   praise the saints
(she'd say)   though I hope I don't get cancer   The pills
erased her mind like a tape: children   grandchildren
all those doilies   vanished as if she had never

pressed them to her breast   Nothing left but pills and tubes

We all need a gardener named Guido to shoot us
before it's too late   When I scratch my wall I try
to scratch it deep   little heaps of powdered cement
along the wall like so many anthills   or mole-
hills   or mountains   it doesn't much matter   does it:
we're talking about meaning here   Outside my cell
the hand is on the throat   the bullet squints in its
chamber   the victory song screeches like a hawk

Roll off the names: Rwanda   Bosnia   Yemen
Waco   Haiti   Cambodia   Los Angeles
No one knows anything   bodies piling up like
anthills   molehills . . .   We may not be able to save
or predict or teach or even please anymore
but at least each line should testify   under oath
under God (undercut   underground):   *we can count*

Quartet

The cello never made it, lost
to us by chance or choice somewhere
between here and there.

We, meanwhile, waited, fiddled
with our instruments, then finally nodded
and began to play without him.

What a strange music—three parts sounded,
one silent, heard only
in the absence of another.

Theology

"I don't believe in God but gravity,"
my father told me, tossing a clod of earth
down the canyon. An arm around my shoulder,
the other sweeping the western panorama,
he said, "This is all too big for God,"
and pared my religious education down
to two subjects: nature and hard work.
I rarely saw him except for those vacations
crammed with hiking, backpacking, climbing,
and cross-country skiing—in short, hard work—
and then he'd return to his 80-hour weeks,
days beginning at four or five A.M.
for forty years, and finally he retired
to unwrap his unwanted gift of idle hours
in a little cabin in the Colorado Rockies,
where if I call I'll find him hammering
up on the roof, among the pine, kneeling
on shingles, each tiny echo of his labor
a kiss against the endless blue sky.

A Short History of Judaic Thought in the Twentieth Century

The rabbis wrote:
although it is forbidden
to touch a dying person,
nevertheless, if the house
catches fire
he must be removed
from the house.

Barbaric!
I say,
and whom may I touch then,
aren't we all
dying?

You smile
your old negotiator's smile
and ask:
but aren't all our houses
burning?

Muse

No angel speaks to me.
And though the wind
plucks the dry leaves
as if they were so many notes
of music, I can hear no words.

Still, I listen. I search
the feathery shapes of clouds
hoping to find the curve of a wing.
And sometimes, when the static
of the world clears just for a moment

a small voice comes through,
chastening. Music
is its own language, it says.
Along the indifferent corridors
of space, angels could be hiding.

The Apple Shrine

Last week you gathered armfuls of apple blossoms
from trees along the roadway, and a few
from the bent Cortland down the street
to place beneath our nameless apple tree
for pollination, you said, so we'd have fruit
next winter. Looking out the window at those rags
and shreds of blossoms beneath the tree,
it could have been a makeshift shrine I saw
in one of those unlikely places where miracles
are said to happen, sightings of angels
or the Virgin, where later ordinary people
place gifts of dolls and colored handkerchiefs.
How fitting, I thought, as if we worshiped
the garden itself, or spring. Just one day later
and equally strange, but fearful

you seemed to lose your vision, went half blind
after work in the garden, for a transgression
not even you with your Science understand.
Healing too is mysterious, the way the seasons
heal each other, one month at a time;
or what can happen in a week in a darkened room
where we both sat thinking about how quickly
everything can change, how thin the crust
of ice we walk on—such thoughts themselves perhaps
a kind of prayer. Today you start to see again,
and I wonder how long we'll remember to be grateful
before we lose ourselves complicitously
in the everyday, waking up surprised one morning
next autumn when for the first time
our tree will be strung with a rosary of apples.

Segovia

For Sergio

*In beholding me Thou givest Thyself to be seen of me, Thou
who art a hidden God.*
— NICHOLAS OF CUSA, DE VISIONE DEI

The shadow in the shiny pilot's jacket,
square as the helipad H at his feet,
cannot yet speak
of night's diurnal residence.
24, he conjures,
rather, anecdotes
that memory movies
among glimpsed thickets—
parables like seeds in the parable.
He stands at the center
of a concrete host
atop a hill in Castille
stripped of blades.

From here Segovia is caught
in the stare of modern lights
that billboard its castle and spires.
The bluffed city is an ancient fish
straddling the rivulets'
difficult throats, lies
on its belly and gazes home
at lead waters that shove themselves away.

The simplest What If's govern his speech.
Imagining peasants and kings
chores a clipped heart
groping for dear theatre.
And like the citadel, he walls,
a recluse in his sureness.

A soldier once, a future man of law,
forever pouring on a stone brow
a grail of losses—a mother buried,
a country served not quite his own,
and mute doubts pressing at the door.

His placid face discards
thoughts not already citizened
within its masonry. I saw
his pupil blur Meninas,
melt the granite of Gaudí
clench at Goya's Saturnine feast.
"Give me jazz and law," he says
while weaving calm tales of jungle battle
and dispensing tactics on seducing women.
His joy pilots twin-engines
across time zones or buries a comrade's ashes
in the sky beneath a dome of cloth.
He folds fearlessness like an old bill
in an older pocket.
But here, in Segovia, he jolts
amid the bony mysteries of a Templar church,
La Vera Cruz, whose twelve sides
and fortressed chapel within
forge another kind of self.

We climbed the inner polygon
to the altar where weapons prayed,
and through its slitted windows,
cross at our backs, mimicked
warrior priests firing
arrows at faith's
faithful enemies. Below us
a chamber like an egg
spreads the whisper of a holy tongue
through the daily poverty of air and space
like loaves and fishes.
In fable the Templars rode two on a horse
beneath the red circle of a cross

against a white field.
They fought Saracens as we do certainty.
Through a bible's landscape of numbers
they mapped God's passage like weather.
Pope and king murdered them in 1312.
Paradox must have no vagaries.

Noah

You have begun to wonder, a glass world
rolling in gentle shadows beneath you,
if all your genuflecting did not turn God
into a masochist. At times, that is the only way
the mighty can feel power, whip in hand,
the red back of the world streaked like Santa Monica
freeway in rush hour. Surely even God,
nameless as the bloated dog floating past,
tires of solitaire with horrors and angels.
Leave it to you, your seasick wife says,
to spoil God. Even He needs a cup of mercy
from strangers met in a stalled elevator.

You are high enough now
to get his attention, call his bluff
a pebble, misname the scoured volcano.
Why, the caldera looks like a dish from here,
a rosy plate delicate with caviar. And the city
a bunch of tossed hats, and the caravan a broken necklace.
True, the many paired hoofs below distract
this moment of reflection. Their racket
is out of place, like bongos in those postwar Paris cafés,
the urgent coughing up its case among smoky rebels
who are tired and want the world to end.

Bent over the railing, you feel your next prayer
should address future dreams of flight.
How men are not made for the vertigo
of solemn trajectories.
You search the earth for a joy: the sight
of a snake pit in the desert.
And that hopeless obedience to need
keeps Him happy.
Even the only ship in a drowned world
can feel like a straitjacket.

The Hollow

For years we scavenged among the dark sands
and ate the moist findings we called bread,
fallen to this ground to teach us
the vertical rules of the spirit.
Above was light and below was hunger.
Even when the wind blew around the few thick trees,
nothing but sand-plated trunks, they could not mark
with what undulations they should the blowing.

And finally we pleased ourselves with a few grunts,
agreeing this meant that, and that meant this.
Soon we learned to sing foreboding.
Because of this and that, a colossus was
on its way because we noticed the shadows
the cliffs threw our way could not be drunk
by the cracked land. So we lived
in those shades and concluded
that our relief from the heat
was love of simple darkness.

It is of no use to disguise our love of shadows.
The colossus will stare mutely
and we will learn to not run from him, we averred.
It turned out to be a horse someone had dreamt.
Our grunts by then had become beliefs.
The dreamer throws images to the horizon
and they fall to the ground as things among beings
who must decipher them. We knocked against its belly,
harder after we were no longer timid.
Nothing. How could we know
it was looking for a wall and memory?

We drew back, took another look
at the sand, the shadows, and we said,
The horse is simply another cliff
even if we cannot live under it.

Who knows why we invented the sacred,
but our punishment came. Forgetting. Swallowing.
Sleeping under the stars, we wanted to call
Night the great shadow.
No one has adored language more than we did then.

Song of Surrender

Hold me close—
            for a night as pure as this
May never return. Stay with me awhile—
For in this birth
Our paths may not cross again.

So what if this tryst
            has no tomorrow.
The dreaded guest is at the door.
When his work is done
I will have drawn my last breath.

Why try to reason
            what is beyond reason?
You bestow upon me more
Than I'm seeking. What little I give
I lavish upon your yearning.

If this will fill
            our begging bowls
Why should laws, oaths, hold us back?
Stretch your arm and take my hand.
History has already written us.

Testament

Consider my state: what I am
surrounded by could be said
to own me. Yet, I could easily give
worldliness the slip, travel barefoot.
Easier still to disclaim the merit
engraved upon my temple: a mere accident
of birth.

The receding hairline is visibly ahead
of a heart yet to break
seed; the surface calm, simply, a foil
for the turmoil within. Lurking
in the shadows, the past
lags behind; the future shows no signs
of catching up.

The history of flesh
is no measure of the soul's uphill
crawl. Inches from oblivion
the heart may yet find its moment
to thaw; in a split
second flood its chambers
with blinding sight.

At the Summit

Milan Cathedral, 1972

For Evelyn Shrifte

A myriad carven statues
known only to the encircling air!
       At uncalculable points
       the profile of some little saint
gazes with bald marble eyes
onto vast indolent Lombardy
       a pair of folded hands prays
       before bright, immediate Heaven,
sandalled feet planted
at the edge of the impossible abyss . . .

This whited world, lonely
as the snowfields of the higher Alps,
       sends with keen incision saintly limbs
       and spires to leap, to shoot,
assault the unsheltered blue,
their glow more glorious
       than that pitiless star,
       the Sun. Daily that orb staggers,
withdraws, dies — a wounded old general
within his tent of night.

But these sweet marble monks,
this youthful angelic population,
       unmelted, unintermittent,
       shines forever.

The Wounded Angel

For Marlene Ekola Gerberick

It fell like a stone from the sky.
It lay in our potato field,
alien, injured, whimpering.
Kain and I dropped our hoes and ran

to see what it was cast down there.
At first all we could see were wings.
Then it—he!—sat up in a tuck.
One wing, broken, hung like a hinge.

When he saw us he dipped his head.
Downcast, his eyes soft as a hare's,
would not meet ours. We saw the blood
on his wonderful white garment.

What must an angel think, falling
through the dazzling air, stunned, surprised
to leave his brothers and sisters,
to land on this ponderous plot?

We tried to talk with him. Nothing.
Finally we decided to act.
We made a litter from bean poles,
carried him to town. He was light.

Not many saw us walking there,
it was the Sabbath—most slept or
were at church. (We'd broken the Word
to dig potatoes, Sunday morn.)

The few that saw us saw a sight:
two stocky boys in dark work clothes,
bearing an angel through the town!
His wings dripped feathers like white rain.

Where to, church father or doctor?
He seemed to be leaving this world.
We stopped before the doctor's stoop;
he took one look and was amazed.

He set to work on surgery,
stitched that wing with strong cat gut,
bathed and dressed the prodigious wounds,
indicated the need for rest.

We left the angel lying there,
on a cot in a dark back room
in a cottage roofed with green grass
in our tiny fishing village.

We returned to our fields, silent
with prayer that he would recover.
Dusk, we returned to the doctor's.
But the shy angel was not there.

The doctor said he'd locked the door
to make sure the patient was safe
from any who might come to pry.
Later, when he unlocked it—gone,

the cot and room unoccupied,
except one feather on the floor,
four feet long, angelically white.
There were no blood spots anywhere.

That was long ago. Kain is dead,
the doctor also. I'm infirm.
"It was some great white bird you saw,"
our wives and villagers chided.

Could that be what happened? Often
Kain and I returned to that field,
scanned the starfields above. Some nights
we stood in a snowstorm all white

as a great floating of feathers.
We felt them brush our face, our soul.
Did we see what we thought we saw?
We hoped to God it might be so.

St. Jacob's Church of the Hanging Hand

He believed that touch
was a simple ride across a stream of velvet
at the skeining stall
or the sting of fire along brazed brass,
or when lightning cooled
in the wet sleep of a valley brook,
he had faith
in the promise of sensation,
the predilection of the body's mortal frame,
subdued, enraged as the hunger moved
to close the spaces
of what seemed to pass
and what, indeed, remained.

But nothing, no one
could predict the draft of terror
invading space so near the tattersall of jewels
the beggar's thumb had grasped.
What miracle of want
had fused his fingers to the Virgin's lace,
as if from an eternity of directions,
a hand or hands in cobra fashion
spiked his wrist,
and gaining force whipped
the venom into feral pitch?

No sooner had he dreamed at dawn
that in the cold posture of prayer,
a soldier's ax had freed his palm,
thought, the conscience vein,
was numbed to infinite suspension.

He remembered how before King Charles lay
in composition for the viewing mass,
he ordered all his fingers

sparred, to keep from being seized,
untombed into the darker death of neglect.
Above the reliquary
the beggar's bone, a deformed winch
propping up the vault of air,
points at the accused avenger. Opposite,
like a feeding plover wading light,
the Virgin, boasting pearls
as high as faith can rise,
tempts the heart of human nature
to face her mirror of greed.
No one breathes.
Should the statue move, all tombs will open.

The Birth of God (from an Early Photograph)

In memoriam, Theodore von Karman

At first silence, a gas or two, a wind unchallenged
as if some breath were conspiring to leap a word
across oblivion. It was to be a universe
of light and sound and calm, ethereal,
a way to mirror a god's mirage through vanity,
but still this wind,

               its whisper like a protest
growing syllables, echoes that would not wane.
It was to be a simple creation. An exercise at most
of mischief, to play at quarks like building blocks,
replenished and diminished, and by its cycle
a god might gain dominion. We would call it nature.
And still this wind,

               a pest, perplexing, by some quirk
of fate escaped the boundaries of imagination.
And worse, it grew aloof, a mind of its own
filled with thoughts of relative notions.
What next, a march, a sit-in, a declaration of rights?
By god, there could be no negotiation.
Until the wind

               had found the future willing,
it named itself HAVOC, and in its wake
propelled the span of the "Galloping Gertie,"
winding her last ride down the ocean narrows.
Above the gimballed truss the gods of intellect convened
as if to find what workings of its mind they failed
to civilize or redeem,

what renegade, what sorcery
of force prepared the eddies of its face,
or since one could not know its face,
that cylindrical, funneled tunnel of eyes
which glowered space like oscillating plumes?
What velocity! What shear flow. What HAVOC wombed,
the gods would overthrow.

Until in boundless words
against the gabled Atheneum like some histrion
Bogarting the Mach abyss of sound, a voice, sudden
as a quantum leap, spoke the syllable of repair,
"wind." "I represent only the wind." And HAVOC
swooned a kiss, and in a mortal gust of whim, married
all of gravity to space.

Thus had God created human nature,
a necessary fiction, like turbulence out of ruins
so passionate even the good lord could not presume.
To the gods of intellect, nothing contained remained
at absolute rest. To man, nothing soared so fickle
as wind and out of reach he wouldn't chase it
to the moon.

After the Funeral

My dream confirms it:
heaven is up,
earth's below.
Housed on his island of clouds,
my father—buried today.

Dropped from above,
a thick two-handed rope.
I have climbed a long way
to enter this picture.
My arms ache.

Reaching over the edge
with his good hand,
he pulls me up.

In the Theatre

Music Box, Chicago

By degree the lights go down
like falling temperatures, the slow
descent of sleep. For the previews,
the ceiling stars stay lit—
small proof there is a world beyond
the screen. The cloud machine pumps airy veils
across the painted sky.

          When the film begins
my life retreats like a bird unseen
beneath the eaves. The actors
are not actors but two angels back on earth.
One is tempted by desire
to stay. The aerialist he seeks
aspires to a higher state
and on that middle plane
they meet.

          In his booth, the projectionist
reads the Sunday *Trib*—the Virgin
has appeared to seven girls
in Yugoslavia. First Lourdes,
he thinks, Fatima and now this.
They see her on a hill behind a house,
in the village church, in uncluttered childhood
where visions are routine. He imagines
pilgrims waiting for the cross to spin,
the sun to change its color,
for simple beads to alchemize.
Glancing at the screen
he sees the shadow of the angel's hand
pass through an actual hand
and thinks of two clocks chiming slightly
out of sync.

Beside me in the flickering dark
a shoulder presses mine—
flesh over bone
resurrects the world again.

As If There Were Only One

In the morning God pulled me onto the porch,
a rain-washed gray and brilliant shore.

I sat in my orange pajamas and waited.
God said, "Look at the tree." And I did.

Its leaves were newly yellow and green,
slick and bright, and so alive it hurt

to take the colors in. My pupils grew
hungry and wide against my will.

God said, "Listen to the tree."
And I did. It said, "Live!"

And it opened itself wider, not with desire,
but the way I imagine a surgeon spreads

the ribs of a patient in distress and rubs
her paralyzed heart, only this tree parted

its own limbs toward the sky—I was the light in that sky.
I reached in to the thick, sweet core

and I lifted it to my mouth and held it there
for a long time until I tasted the word

"tree" (because I had forgotten its name).
Then I said my own name twice softly.

Augustine said, *God loves each of us as if
there were only one of us*, but I hadn't believed him.

And God put me down on the steps with my coffee
and my cigarettes. And, although I still

could not eat nor sleep, that evening
and that morning were my first day back.

Finishing Touch

Ever since the painter depicted
Your finger extended to Your creature,

we have known we crave a surrogate touch.
We press others' palms to our faces,

as if we were still being molded,
polished by an apprenticed love revising

our rougher destinies: Each hand found
more skillful than the last, each imprint closer

to Your transforming seal. I know this,
and still I have to ask for reprieve

in illusion, to linger in this present
flesh, believe in her finishing touch.

I want *this* hand: its knowing strokes
inside my thighs where all portrayal begins.

Let this hand complete me for the stretch,
the soft edges of these fingers be the last

of earth I feel, let it be her own
hand—hers alone—that will close these eyes.

Faith in Florida

First month in Florida I couldn't get used
to the lizards, scuttling across my driveway

and my garden, startling me in my kitchen,
swiping their tails in determined retreat.

Then I decided they were manifestations
of divine presence—now we get on fine.

I would even say they comfort me.
Their thrashing through the leaves sounds like wings

beating into sudden flight. My father,
on the gray porch of the house on Crescent

Boulevard, the house where he was born,
had me talking to lizards when I was five

or so. *Lizard, lizard, show me your penny*,
and their throats opened to a bright red disc.

It was like magic. He spoke the words again,
and again they obeyed, blasting their round red

trumpets. (My grandmother told me alligators
swam in her ivy sea to keep me up on the steps.)

Without my father around, I have both to conjure
and to believe my own stories, perhaps as he

learned to do without her, fiercely call *proof*
the signs we know have been there all along.

Illumination

As if some monk bored
in the cold scriptorium
had let his quill

wander from the morning
Gospel, two tendrils
of wisteria

have scrolled
their green fervour
into the weave of a wicker

deck chair to whisper
with each spiral,
every sweet leaf

and dew sparkle,
Brother, come
with us, come home.

Teresa

For Seán Dunne

Say *darkness*, say *light*. The eagle
and the dove. I walked the meadow,
an unshod Carmelite in Castile.
I was ill often, kneeling
in the garden to forget Spanish
pillage in America, curses
from the Alhambra, Rome's
rigorous encyclicals, and my
own painful self-loathing. I
whispered to Him. I fell down
amid the asters, woodbine, pale
lemongrass, and He came to me,
a bright lance, an aria, lightning.
Wing of shadow, an ivory wing:
it was ecstasy, fulfillment, tremolo
of contrition. I have written
since in Avila's sun, in my cell
or the kitchen, of that sweet spiral,
the cast lance. *The Interior
Castle, Book of Foundations*: my
commonsense confessions. But
it was never a voice, understand,
never instruction. Just vibrato
without sound, an unsexual trembling,
till I felt Christ's eagle lifting
me in his talons. Entering a flurry
of heavenly petals, I saw how
trees, dark stalks, stonecrops,
and the very shadows become
scripture falling across the snow.

The Poet Is Like a Church

The poet is like a church, an abandoned one,
with a ruined cemetery and swishing
cypress trees. The poet is like a burlap bag
thrown over a "priceless work of art";
the shape of the bag in half-light becomes
itself a work of art; the texture, the smell
of burlap appeal more tumultuously
to the senses than any marbled hall
in all the great museums. The poet is like
a hot shower after a hot bath, like smoke
from a teenager's surreptitious cigarette,
like the stolid geometrician who,
unaccountably, decides to deliver
his conference paper wearing wraparound shades.

The Annunciation

After the painting by D. G. Rossetti

Surely God thought this would be a moment
      to celebrate: an angel come down
in long white robes trumpeting
      divine maternity. But Mary, freshly
waked, cringes against the wall, pulling
      the sheets up to her chin. She seems
to regard the lily offered her, sweet-smelling
      though it may be, as meager reward
for so much responsibility. The angel
      looks disillusioned. He'd expected
to be greeted like a suitor; instead,
      he's brought all that light to bear
on the pale sharp face of a bony girl
      with hollow, profoundly reluctant eyes.

History

Burst of passion skims
the forest, nudges ancient
trees that shaded monks

and messengers from raw
ephemeral kingdoms. Who
choked on cockled dreams

outlined with sedge and moss,
crude cycles of the masks
of power and storm. Stiff-

armed predators who slipped
out of the waves and came
to this. Seduced the colors

of the sky, the earth, bent
sound, willed thought to
claim existence for themselves.

And as the bees tucked into
mouths of rhododendrons
waited to steal their gold.

Enough:

After a restless night, dreams
of an age gone mad, where even

poets could turn a deaf ear to
the savagery, write of Greek gods

in surreal tongues, while stokers
sifted for gold teeth among their

victims' ashes, I stare, clench-
jawed, into the last dregs of my

tea-stained, pint-size Denby breakfast
cup, pinpoint a landscape thirsting

for a flower. Breathe deep, spit
out the bitter taste of memory,

and see why, overwhelmed by pain,
Van Gogh found solace in sunflowers.

Indian Things

How come you don't write more about eagles,
tipis, Mother Earth . . . you know, Indian things?
This poem is not about
praying to circling eagles.
This poem is about
the soaring poet who moves
me to my knees. Mick Vranich,
hidden in that secret forest
deep in the rusty
heart of Detroit. He perches
in the swaying trees.
His long black wings
toll the sonic bell of his Fender
Stratocaster. His voice like a saw
cross-cuts the darkening sky,
his voice like a hammer
nails and raises the shape of a roof
over the wounded
flesh of the world.
This poem is not about
walking with spirits of deer.
This poem is about
the woman who speaks
tongue of birds. My wife
wanders in the juniper
meadow, dew glistening
in her singing hair. She calls
hawks by secret names.
Her sharp shiny eye
sees every flicker of tail in grass,
feather in sky. Her scent like wine
drunkens the wings of butterflies.
She winks at the laughing black
salamander, smiles at the snakes
who rub soft bellies

on her bare feet.
This poem is not about
the sacred shape of a tipi.
This poem is about
the fragile house of a man's
ancient chest. My father,
forever impatient, stands
in line at the Department
of Motor Vehicles. He waits
to pass one last secret test.
His worn aching heart
sputters, throws him to the tiled
floor. His gaze fixes on the cold,
white ceiling light and he smiles.
He imagines he is behind the wheel,
driving one thousand miles
to make peace
with a distant son.
This poem is not about
being born of Mother Earth.
This poem is about
the woman who first gave
blood to my heart. My mother,
drifting in a rocking chair
within the creaking quiet
walls of her room. She counts
secrets, days as miracles.
Her small tired fingers stroke
blue flowers on her favorite
sweater. Her dreams like holy waters
wash away her muddy memory.
She blinks at the snowy television
screen where the fuzzy
face of Jesus grins,
forgives her only sin,
me and other Indian things.

Spare Tire

(the atheist's unmailed letter to god)

I've intended to be harder, to refuse your body in the
    storms
and spit at the magnetic voice over my sky when I've been
    wasted,
to sneak out on you in the evening, sneak out on you and
    sell myself,
have my dress torn and make it my bed.
I've intended to inject you into the vein I tap every
    morning,
a liquid hot enough to boil your laughter,
I've intended to crush what is still optimistic within you,
before you begin to share it, before abundance, pity,
before the horizon is thought of something we both
    understand.
I've intended, improvised, prayed to do you wrong,
be weak, cowardly, display that frown which cries
how convoluted the flesh is, what a rabid pest,
what an ugly duck, but I don't have that frown
or impotence, I'm still awed by your seasons,
contradicted by your vivacity.
I still hate you in the contemporary, Freudian way.

A shoreless bath a fabulous boast

like a dowry like a razzle-dazzle
and a thirst left by two feuds
I am the fear of the attic
I am the sharp edge of the rivers
I am the fume of the armaments I am the bellicose land
I am not your friend nor am I a fanatic
I am not the water of easy communions
I want I shall be a servant of the light
which will not bend
before passion before cold.
I resist my light out of stupidity
and often choose to draw with India ink
and when I wake up
I reach for bodies which
in matter press out their shore.

I am not an Amazon — a warrior,

nor am I a mother.
I am a leaf of surrender and joy
who does not need another
to be one.
I am a Goddess like you
I am a bath of balm
I am a river as much as an ocean.
I am a steel mill of passion
I am a child of the virgin forests
I am the faith of rain
transforming into steam as clean
as heaven itself.
I am the innocence of spring
offering again its buds.
I do not keep dependents, opponents or crowds.
I am a starry child, a woman in love.

Divine Will

For M., in Romania

Seven hours: late afternoon here, lightning
    stuttering the clocks, the stunned
        air a bronze bell one tick
        past tolling—but already midnight
at the café where you're sipping vodka
    with your former lover who's grown
        impatient with abundance:
        the foil-wrapped chocolates, icy heaps
of scallops, thousand cereals, & Borgesian
    library of toilet papers, blue & yellow,
        beyond wobbly pyramids of avocado
        fluorescing the supermarket where we shop.
You've mentioned me only once, though
    smoke-plumes loitering near the stuck
        ceiling fan assume foreplay in his gaze,
    so he smudges one last cigarette onto the tabletop.
Seven hours: despite this sporadic flickering,
    I'm still reading—the unsurprisingly
        brief biography of Luisa Piccareta,
    Little Daughter of the Divine Will
b. Corato, Italy 1882 d. Corato, Italy 1947
    who survived on nothing but Communion
        wafers for sixty-five years.
    "She lived in her bed, and died each day.
Each day, in order for her to return to life,
    a priest had to come—usually
        one of her five confessors—
    to give her the order to obey him
and return to life." The lamplight fails,
    then flares. Hummingbird feeders
        twist among black branches,
    then dangle like gaudy fishhooks.
Your sullen ex watches as you slip

two dollars under the empty
      ashtray, then crumple them back,
   embarrassed by your mistake, before
fingering the still-familiar lei.
   We tender ourselves to a will
      less divine, hurly-burly,
      here & there, floats & solutions.
Seven hours: soon you'll fly west, erasing
   the difference, cradling in your skirt
      six hollow eggs, airy gifts,
   hand-painted for the Orthodox Easter.

The Conversion of Saint Paul

In 1956 I was the shepherd boy
with nothing to offer the infant Jesus.

Kissed goodbye, I left the walk-up
in a white, ankle-length, terrycloth robe,

flailing my grandfather's wooden cane
wrapped from crook to tip in foil.

Secretaries stared from passing buses
at this Biblical apparition

leading his invisible sheep to school,
O little, wild-eyed prophet of Brooklyn!

Older, I portrayed the leper
gifted with half of St. Martin's cloak

and, with paper arrows and red Play-Doh,
evoked the passion of St. Sebastian.

Then I had to fake a terrible fall
to honor the conversion of St. Paul—

when I changed into costume
in the boys' musty coatroom,

Sister Euphrasia knelt to hike
the elastic waistband of my briefs

to better arrange my torn-sheet toga.
In second grade, this ageless ogre

had pasted Easter seals on my skull
and locked me in a cobwebbed cubicle,

pretending to air-mail me to China
where I'd never again see my mother!

Funny enough today, I guess,
but then I pleaded for forgiveness.

Now her sour breath flushed my face
when — classmates clamoring their impatience —

she whispered Jesus
would be judging my performance,

then thrust me from her failing sight
to be apprehended by all that light.

What We Believe

Jesus was not the Son of God. He was a yogi
who tranced out on the cross — a fanatic like Jim
Jones or David Koresch, with better publicity.

President Kennedy was killed by the Cubans,
the Russians, the C.I.A.; Lee Harvey Oswald
was paid to take the fall. A group of evil

scientists created AIDS to wipe out Blacks,
dope addicts, homosexuals. Drug companies
quash cures to keep their profits high.

God is a Big Man with a white beard who sees us
when we're sleeping, who knows when we're awake.
There is no God; there's just Physics, which couldn't

care less if a sparrow falls. Ours is the greatest,
best-governed country in the world, and needs
a top-to-bottom overhaul. Rodney King was high

on angel dust when the cops beat him.
He'd learned, in jail, a way to leap up
from the ground and break a cop's neck instantly.

O. J. Simpson was framed by the L.A.P.D.
Laws are made to keep the powerful that way.
Religions are all superstition except ours.

Democracies and dictatorships, coups and counter-
coups are smoke-screens. Corporations rule.
The letters in our names control our lives.

A New Mexico army base hides the remains
of crashed space aliens. They have large heads,
small bodies, glowing eyes. They're linked

to human evolution, ancient Egypt, the Flood,
Easter Island, Incas, Aztecs, Mayans, and the Deficit.
Their ship is made of silvery metal impervious

to any force on earth. They want either to save us
from ourselves, or to destroy us utterly.
Everything worked better in the Golden Age.

Identifying with the Buddha

We forget, praising his lotus feet, that he named his son Rahula:
  "Fetter" or "Impediment."
This would seem cruel from anyone not vanquishing the fires of
  Lust, Hate, and Delusion —
especially when *his* parents named him Siddhartha: "Whose Aim
  Is Accomplished."

We fault others for naming children Ima Hogg, Ben Dover, Isabel
  Ringing,
knowing that Queen Latifah or Majestyk Magnyfycent will more likely
  shine than Debit, Ordure, Angina.
Consider John Graves the mortician; Fred Carie, the dentist; Lydia
  Spies, the paranoid —

yet "Rahula" is seen as just and wise, as is the fact that, 29, Siddhartha
  abandoned his wife and Impediment.
My granddad did that, and his name became a curse. Since no one calls
  Siddhartha *selfish, mean,* a *deadbeat dad,*
why badmouth me for naming St. Luke's pastor "Bore," my rich
  maiden aunt "Windfall,"

my demented mom "Millstone"? Her given name was much plainer
  than Mahamaya —
Mary Sue — and before my birth she didn't dream a silver elephant
  entered through her side,
as Siddhartha's mother did; still, at eight pounds five ounces, I felt
  like an elephant, she said.

After three miscarriages, my mother dreamed of holding a healthy child,
    and didn't care
if it grew up to enumerate the Four Noble Truths and reach nirvana,
    or become a shoeshine boy.
She didn't fall prostrate, but she worshipped me, instilling the sense
    of lovability

that lets me be, sometimes, a mean son-of-a-bitch. Hey, you monks
    with tinkling bells,
orange robes, shaved heads—why not sculpt stone statues of me?
    Why not build gold temples to me,
and carve wooden figures of me whose stomach (kept flat with situps
    and crunches) you rub for luck?

Why not revere me, and everyone with enough guts to call a fetter
    a fetter, enough spunk
to boot a Pekingese—yapping like Mara the Devil—when its owner's
    back is turned?
Siddhartha mortified the flesh until he looked like Uncle Rictus
    on *Tales from the Crypt,*

but didn't reach enlightenment until he ate well-balanced meals,
    and kicked back
in the shade of a Bo tree. I say it's trying to be so good, wise, pure,
    and self-denying
that's the real *rahula.* I say attachment to our virtuous suffering
    keeps us chipping teeth on,

bloodying wrists and ankles against, howling prayers and praises
    to our chains.
I say forget the old Buddha and follow me, or if not me, then
    the Pierces from Pacoima—
Dick and Patti—who work as a bus driver and grocery checker
    respectively,

drink too much, have put on weight, bicker about money and sex,
    but managed,
when Patti had twins—red, wrinkled, squalling bulletheads—
    to name one Celeste,
"heavenly," and the other David, "beloved."

Faith

Mom told me how she "worked on" hers
(like an old car?), how it felt "strong today"
(like a weightlifter?), how it could "raise
the dead" (an elevator full of bones?).

I'd earned a Bible by not missing Sunday
school. Slogging through *thous* and *thines*,
makests and *takests* and *begats*,
I pictured heaven as clouds, harps, angels,

Pearly Gates behind which we would live—
Mom, Dad, Susie, and me, a crewcut 8—
for "all eternity." My faith, like my fastball,
seemed naturally strong. Not faith in Jesus

who, no matter how I prayed, never came
to drive off monsters (his halo a perfect
night light), never met me in the woods
to help build forts or catch copperheads—

I had faith in Mom, who said that Jesus
cherished me, that good deeds were gold
in heaven, that everyone we loved
would greet us on that distant day we died,

when pain and sadness would "fall from us
like rags." "God's grace will wash us clean,"
she still insisted as she bathed and fed my dad,
changed his diaper and read to him

from the Book of Job six years after his stroke.
For the last three, she prayed that God
would "call home" his moaning, mindless husk—
prayed the way she prays now,

blind and deaf, thrashing and raving
in "Serenity Home," braying and squalling,
"Come for me, Jesus!" And no one comes.
"God have mercy on me!" And there is none.

Amaryllis

After Rilke

You've seen a cat consume a hummingbird, seen
it scoop its beating body from the pyrocanthus bush
and break its wings with tufted paws
before marshaling it, whole, into its bone-tough throat;
seen a boy, heart racing with cocaine, climb
from a car window in a tumble to the ground,
his search for pleasure ending in skinned palms;
a woman's shouts as she is pushed into the police cruiser,
large hand pressing her head into the door,
red lights spinning their tornado in the street.

But all of that will fade; on the table is the amaryllis,
pushing its monstrous body in the air,
requiring no soil to do so, having wound
two seasons' rot into a white and papered bulb,
exacting nutrition from the winter light,
culling from complex chemistry the tints
and fragments that tissue and pause and build
again the pigment and filament.
The flower crescendos, toward the light,
though better to say despite it,
gores through gorse and pebble
to form a throat, so breakable, open
with its tender pistils, damp with rosin,
simple in its simple sex, to burn and siphon
itself in air. Tongue of fire, tongue
of earth, the amaryllis is the rudiment
of form itself, forming its meretricious petals
to trumpet and exclaim.

How you admire it. How you see it vibrate
in the draft, a song it is, a complex wheel
bitten with cogs, swelling and sexual,

though nothing will touch it. You have forced it
to spread itself, to cleave and grasp,
remorseless, open to your assignments—
this is availability, this is tenderness,
this red plane is given to the world.
Sometimes the heart breaks. Sometimes
it is not held hostage. The red world
where cells prepare for the unexpected
splays open at the window's ledge.
Be not human you inhuman thing.
No anxious, no foible, no hesitating hand.
Pry with fiber your course through sand,
point your whole body toward the unknown
away from the dead.
Be water and light and land,
no contrivance, no gasp, no dream
where there is no head.

Difficult Body

A story: There was a cow in the road, struck by a semi—
half-moon of carcass and jutting legs, eyes
already milky with dust and snow, rolled upward

as if tired of this world tilted on its side.
We drove through the pink light of the police cruiser
her broken flank blowing steam in the air.

Minutes later, a deer sprang onto the road
and we hit her, crushed her pelvis—the drama reversed,
first consequence, then action—but the doe,

not dead, pulled herself with front legs
into the ditch. My father went to her, stunned her
with a tire iron before cutting her throat, and today I think

of the body of St. Francis in the Arizona desert,
carved from wood and laid in his casket,
lovingly dressed in red and white satin

covered in petitions—medals, locks of hair,
photos of infants, his head lifted and stroked,
the grain of his brow kissed by the penitent.

O wooden saint, dry body. I will not be like you,
carapace. A chalky shell scooped of its life.
I will leave less than this behind me.

Contributors' Notes

DAVID BAKER is the author of eight books, most recently *Heresy and the Ideal: On Contemporary Poetry* and *Changeable Thunder*. His work has appeared in many magazines, such as the *Atlantic*, the *Nation*, the *New Yorker*, and *Poetry*, and he has won awards and fellowships from the National Endowment for the Arts, Society of Midland Authors, Poetry Society of America, and elsewhere. Baker is professor of English at Denison University and poetry editor of the *Kenyon Review*.

JACK BEDELL was born and raised in Houma, Louisiana, in 1966. He holds B.A. and M.A. degrees from Northwestern State University in Natchitoches, Louisiana, an M.F.A. in poetry from the University of Arkansas–Fayetteville, and a Ph.D. in English/creative writing from the University of Louisiana–Lafayette. Currently he is an associate professor of English at Southeastern Louisiana State University where he also serves as editor of *Louisiana Literature*. He is the author of two books of poetry, and his writing has appeared in *Critique, Hudson Review, Negative Capability, Southern Humanities Review*, and *West Branch*.

MARVIN BELL was born in New York City in 1937 and grew up on rural Long Island. He holds a bachelor's degree from Alfred University, a master's degree from the University of Chicago, and a Master of Fine Arts degree from the University of Iowa. He is the author of fifteen books of poetry, including *Stars Which See, Stars Which Do Not See*, which was a finalist for the National Book Award, and *Probably Volume of Dreams*, which was a Lamont Poetry Selection of the Academy of American Poets. His honors include the American Academy of Arts and Letters Award in Literature, Guggenheim, and National Endowment for the Arts fellowships, and Senior Fulbright appointments to Yugoslavia and Australia. He is a longtime member of the faculty of the University of Iowa Writers' Workshop, where he is the Flannery O'Connor Professor of Letters.

J. J. BLICKSTEIN is a native New Yorker, poet/visual artist, and the editor of *Hunger Magazine*. His writing has appeared in *Fish Drum, Heavenbone, Long Shot*, and *Rattle*, as well as the poetry anthologies *Poet's Gallery Press* and *American Diaspora: Poetry of Displacement*.

BRUCE BOND is the author of four books of poetry, including *The Throats of Narcissus*. He has received fellowships from the National Endowment for the Arts, the Texas Commission on the Arts, the Breadloaf Writers' Conference, the Wesleyan Writers' Conference, MacDowell, Yaddo, the Sewanee Writers' conference, and other organizations. Presently he is director of creative writing at the

University of North Texas and poetry editor for the *American Literary Review*.

DARRELL BOURQUE is head of the English Department at the University of Louisiana where he is the Friends of the Humanities/Board of Regents Endowed Professor. His poetry publications include *Plainsongs* and *Burnt Water Suite*.

GAYLORD BREWER is an associate professor at Middle Tennessee State University, where he founded and edits *Poems and Plays*. His publications include *David Mamet and Film*, *Charles Bukowski*, and four collections of poems, including *Devilfish* and *Four Nails*.

MAXINE CHERNOFF is the author of five books of poetry and five books of fiction. She is professor of creative writing at San Francisco State University and editor with Paul Hoover of the journal *New American Writing*. She has read from her work in Australia, Belgium, Germany, England, and Scotland.

MARTHA COLLINS is the author of four volumes of poetry, most recently *Some Things Words Can Do*. She has also cotranslated and published, with the author, *The Women Carry River Water*, the Vietnamese poems of Nguyen Quang Thieu. She is the Pauline Delaney Professor of Creative Writing at Oberlin College, where she also serves as an editor of *Field*.

NICOLE COOLEY grew up in New Orleans, Louisiana. She received her B.A. from Brown University, her M.F.A. from the Iowa Writers' Workshop, and her Ph.D. from Emory University. She is the author of *Resurrection*, which was chosen by Cynthia MacDonald to receive the 1995 Walt Whitman Award. Her poems have appeared in *Poetry*, *Field*, *Poetry Northwest*, *Ploughshares*, and the *Nation*. She won a "Discovery"/*The Nation* Award for her poetry in 1994, and in 1996 she received a fiction grant from the National Endowment for the Arts. She taught at Bucknell University before accepting a position to teach creative writing at Queens College–CUNY. In 1998, HarperCollins published her novel *Judy Garland, Ginger Love*. Cooley currently lives in New York City and is working on a book of poetry about the Salem witch trials of 1692, titled *The Afflicted Girls*.

PETER COOLEY was born in Detroit and grew up there and in the suburbs of the city. A graduate of Shimer College, the University of Chicago, and the University of Iowa, where he was a student in the Writers' Workshop and received his Ph.D., he is currently professor of English at Tulane University in New Orleans teaching creative writing. Married and the father of three children, he has published six books of poetry: *The Company of Strangers*, *The Room Where the Summer Ends*, *Nightseasons*, *The Van Gogh Notebook*, *The Astonished Hours*, and *Sacred Conversations*.

ROBERT DANA's most recent books of poetry are *Summer* and *Hello, Stranger*. He also edited *A Community of Writers: Paul Engle and the*

Iowa Writer's Workshop. Dana graduated in 1954 from the University of Iowa Writers' Workshop where he studied with Robert Lowell and John Berryman. He has served as Distinguished Visiting Writer at universities in the United States and abroad; after forty years of teaching at Cornell College he retired in 1994 as professor of English and poet-in-residence. His work was awarded National Endowment fellowships in 1985 and 1993, the Delmore Schwartz Memorial Poetry Award in 1989, and a Pushcart Prize in 1996.

CHRISTOPHER DAVIS was born in 1960 in Whittier, California, received a B.A. in English from Syracuse University and an M.F.A. from the Iowa Writers' Workshop, and is currently associate professor of creative writing at the University of North Carolina–Charlotte. His first collection of poetry, *The Tyrant of the Past and the Slave of the Future*, won the 1988 Associated Writing Programs Award, and his second, *The Patriot*, won the 1998 University of Georgia Press Contemporary Poetry Series competition. His third collection will be called *A History of the Only War*, and poems that will be included in the manuscript have appeared in many journals, including *Harvard Review*, *Denver Quarterly*, *Boston Book Review*, *Pequod*, *Massachusetts Review*, *Volt*, *Fence*, and others.

CHARD DENIORD's poems have appeared recently in *Witness*, *The Pushcart Prize XXII*, *The Best American Poetry 1999*, the *Gettysburg Review*, the *Iowa Review*, *Agni*, the *Harvard Review*, and *Ploughshares*. He is the author of *Asleep in the Fire*. He teaches English and creative writing at Providence College.

STEPHEN DUNN is the author of eleven collections of poetry, including *Different Hours* and *Loosestrife* (National Book Critics Circle Award finalist, 1996). Other books include *New and Selected Poems: 1974–1994*, *Landscape at the End of the Century*, *Between Angels*, and *Riffs and Reciprocities: Prose Pairs*. *Local Time* was a winner of the National Poetry Series in 1986. Four other poetry collections were published and a new and expanded version of *Walking Light: Memoirs and Essays on Poetry* was issued in 2001. Dunn is Distinguished Professor of Creative Writing at Richard Stockton College of New Jersey.

MARTÍN ESPADA, a Puerto Rican who was born in Brooklyn, has won two fellowships from the National Endowment for the Arts, a Massachusetts Artists' Fellowship, the PEN/Revson Fellowship, and the Paterson Poetry Prize. In addition to writing poetry and teaching at the University of Massachusetts, Espada has been a tenant lawyer in Chelsea, Massachusetts, a factory worker, and the desk clerk on the night shift at a transient hotel. He also regularly volunteers his time to work with disadvantaged children in cities surrounding the university such as Holyoke, Springfield, and Hartford. His newest poetry collection is *A Mayan Astronomer in Hell's Kitchen*.

RICHARD FOERSTER was born in the Bronx, New York, and attended
Fordham University and the University of Virginia. He is the author of
four poetry collections: *Sudden Harbor*; *Patterns of Descent*; *Trillium*,
which received honorable mention for the 2000 Poets' Prize; and
Double Going. Other honors include the "Discovery"/*The Nation*
Award, *Poetry*'s Bess Hokin Prize, fellowships from the National
Endowment for the Arts and the Maine Arts Commission, and the
2000/2001 Amy Lowell Poetry Traveling Scholarship. He has
worked as a lexicographer, educational writer, typesetter, and as the
editor of the literary magazine *Chelsea*. He currently lives in York
Beach, Maine.

REGINALD GIBBONS's most recent books of poems are *Sparrow: New and
Selected Poems*, which won the 1998 Balcones Poetry Prize, and
Homage to Longshot O'Leary. A paperback edition of his novel
Sweetbitter was issued in 1996 and his translation of Euripides's
Bakkhai is forthcoming. From 1981 till 1997 he was the editor of
TriQuarterly magazine at Northwestern University, where he is
currently a professor of English.

DANA GIOIA's essays and criticism have appeared in many periodicals,
including the *Nation*, the *New Yorker*, and the *Atlantic*. He is a
translator and anthologist of Italian poetry, as well as the author of
three poetry collections. His critical collection, *Can Poetry Matter?* was
a finalist for the 1992 National Book Critics Circle Award. He has
recently completed the libretto for *Nosferatu*, an opera by Alva
Henderson.

SUSAN HAHN is the author of five poetry collections and she serves as
editor of *TriQuarterly*. Her first play was performed in April 2000 at
Victory Gardens Theater as part of their New Playwrights 2000
Festival. She is the recipient of numerous awards for poetry including
the Society of Midland Authors Award, the George Kent Prize from
Poetry, and many Illinois Arts Council awards.

BOB HICOK is the author of three poetry collections, including *Animal
Soul*, which was a finalist for the 2001 National Book Critics Circle
Award. An N.E.A. Fellow for 1999, his poetry has appeared in *The Best
American Poetry* (1997 and 1999), and two Pushcart Prize anthologies.
He owns an automotive die design business.

ADAM HILL's poems have appeared in the *American Poetry Review*,
Poetry Northwest, and the *Seattle Review*. He currently teaches
literature and writing at California Polytechnic State University–
San Luis Obispo.

PAUL HOOVER is author of seven poetry collections, including *Totem and
Shadow: New and Selected Poems*; *Viridian*; *The Novel: A Poem*; and
Idea, which won the Carl Sandburg Award given by Friends of the
Chicago Public Library. His poetry has appeared in *American Poetry
Review*, the *New Republic*, the *Paris Review*, *Sulfur*, *Conjunctions*,

TriQuarterly, and *Partisan Review*, among others. It has also been included in five editions of the annual anthology *The Best American Poetry*. He is editor of a major anthology, *Postmodern American Poetry*, and edits with Maxine Chernoff the literary magazine *New American Writing*.

PETER JOHNSON was born in Buffalo, New York, in 1951. He received his B.A. from SUNY–Buffalo, and his M.A. and Ph.D. in English from the University of New Hampshire. He is the winner of the 2001 James Laughlin Award for his second collection of prose poems, *Miracles and Mortifications*. His previous books include the chapbook *Love Poems for the Millennium*; *I'm a Man*, winner of Raincrow Press's Fiction Chapbook Contest; and the poetry collection *Pretty Happy!* Johnson is the founder and editor of *The Prose Poem: An International Journal*. A contributing editor to *American Poetry Review*, *Web del Sol*, and *Slope*, Johnson teaches creative writing and children's literature at Providence College in Rhode Island.

ALICE JONES's books include *The Knot*, winner of the 1992 Beatrice Hawley Award from Alice James Books, and *Anatomy*, a letterpress chapbook from Bullnettle Press of San Francisco. Her poems have appeared in *Chelsea*, *Denver Quarterly*, the *Harvard Review*, *Ploughshares*, and *The Best American Poetry of 1994*, and she has received fellowships from the Bread Loaf Writers' Conference as well as the National Endowment for the Arts.

GEORGE KALAMARAS is the author of *The Theory and Function of Mangoes*, a collection of poems that won the Four Way Books 1998 Intro Series in Poetry Award, and *Reclaiming the Tacit Dimension: Symbolic Form in the Rhetoric of Silence*, a study of Hindu mysticism and Western composition theory. His poems have appeared in many anthologies and journals, including *The Best American Poetry 1997*. He is the recipient of a 1993 National Endowment for the Arts Creative Writing Fellowship and the *Abiko Quarterly* (Japan) International Poetry Prize. A longtime practitioner of yogic meditation, he spent several months during 1994 in India on an Indo-U.S. Advanced Research Fellowship from the Fulbright Foundation and the Indo-U.S. Subcommission on Education and Culture. Born in Chicago, Kalamaras received his doctorate from the University at Albany and currently is an associate professor of English at Indiana University–Purdue University Fort Wayne.

JARRET KEENE, born in 1973, is the son of a Tampa firefighter and a Cuban schoolteacher. He is author of a poetry collection, *Monster Fashion*. His Pushcart-nominated stories, essays, and verse have appeared in *American Literary Review*, the *Carolina Quarterly*, the *Greensboro Review*, *New England Review*, and *Utne Reader*. He teaches creative writing and literature at the University of Nevada–Las Vegas and is an art and entertainment writer for the *Las Vegas*

Mercury. Keene also is editor for the literary journal *Black Box Recording*.

CAROLYN KIZER has published eight books of poetry, two books of criticism, and a book of translations. She edited *The Essential John Clare* and *100 Great Poems by Women*. Her book, *Yin*, won the Pulitzer Prize in 1985. Other honors and awards are from the National Academy of Arts and Letters, the Poetry Society of America, and the Theodore Roethke Foundation, as well as the Aiken Taylor Prize. Her poems are included in the last five years of *The Best American Poetry* series. She was the first director of literature for the National Endowment for the Arts. The *San Francisco Chronicle* has called her a National Treasure.

KO WON is the author of more than a dozen books, including *The Turn of Zero* and *Voices in Diversity*. He studied English literature at Queen Mary College, University of London, earned his M.F.A. in creative writing from the University of Iowa, and his Ph.D. in comparative literature from N.Y.U. He taught at Brooklyn College, the City University of New York, and the University of California, Riverside; he currently teaches at the University of La Verne in California.

SYDNEY LEA is the author of seven poetry collections, including *To the Bone: New and Selected Poems* and *Pursuit of a Wound*. His only novel, *A Place in Mind*, was first published in 1989 and in paperback in 1997. Lea was the founder and longtime editor of the *New England Review*. He is the past recipient of a Guggenheim Fellowship for poetry and of a Rockefeller Foundation Fellowship. A Vermont native, Lea is also the author of numerous essays and magazine pieces on morally responsible hunting and dog training, some of which are collected in *Hunting the Whole Way Home*.

LI-YOUNG LEE was born in 1957 in Jakarta, Indonesia, of Chinese parents. He attended the Universities of Pittsburgh and Arizona and the State University of New York at Brockport. He has taught at several universities, including Northwestern and the University of Iowa. He is the author of *Book of My Nights*; *The City in Which I Love You*, which was the 1990 Lamont Poetry Selection; and *Rose*, which won the Delmore Schwartz Memorial Poetry Award; as well as a memoir entitled *The Winged Seed: A Remembrance*, which received an American Book Award from the Before Columbus Foundation. His other honors include a Lannan Literary Award, a Whiting Writer's Award, grants from the Illinois Arts Council, the Commonwealth of Pennsylvania, the Pennsylvania Council on the Arts, and the National Endowment for the Arts, and a Guggenheim Foundation fellowship. He lives in Chicago.

PETER MEINKE is the author of eleven books of poetry, including *Zinc Fingers: New and Selected Poems* and *Scars*. His poems have appeared in *Poetry*, the *New Yorker*, the *Atlantic*, the *Georgia Review*, and scores of other magazines and publications. Among his many awards are the Olivet Prize, the Paumanok Award, three prizes from the Poetry Society of America, two N.E.A. fellowships in poetry, and the Flannery O'Connor Award for his short story collection, *The Piano Tuner*. Meinke lives in St. Petersburg, Florida.

LEONARD NATHAN is the author of nine volumes of poetry including *The Potato Eaters* and *Returning Your Call*, which was nominated for the National Book Award in poetry in 1976. He has received the National Institute of Arts and Letters prize for poetry and a Guggenheim Fellowship, among many other awards and honors. He lives in Kensington, California.

RICHARD NEWMAN's poetry and essays have recently appeared in *Black Dirt, Boulevard, Crab Orchard Review, Slant, Southern Humanities Review, Spoon River Poetry Review*, and others. He edits *River Styx* in St. Louis, Missouri.

LINDA PASTAN is the author of ten volumes of poetry, including *Carnival Evening: New and Selected Poems 1968–1998*, which was a finalist for the National Book Award. She was poet laureate of Maryland from 1991 to 1995, and has been on staff at the Bread Loaf Writers' Conference for twenty years. Among her many awards are the Dylan Thomas Award, the Di Castagnola Award, the Bess Hokin Prize of *Poetry*, the Virginia Faulkner Award from *Prairie Schooner*, and a Pushcart Prize.

RICARDO PAU-LLOSA is the author of five poetry collections, including *The Mastery Impulse* and *Vereda Tropical*. His poems and short stories have been published widely. An internationally renowned art critic, he has written extensively on the visual arts, specializing in twentieth-century Latin American painting and sculpture.

SALEEM PEERADINA has master's degrees in English from Bombay University and Wake Forest University. He is the author of two books of poetry, *First Offence* and *Group Portrait*, and he has edited several anthologies of poetry such as *Contemporary Indian Poetry in English: An Assessment and Selection*, one of the earliest and most widely used books throughout the Commonwealth, particularly in courses on Indian writing in English. Currently, Peeradina is an associate professor of English at Siena Heights University.

ROBERT PHILLIPS's fifth collection of poetry, *Breakdown Lane*, has gone into its second printing and his sixth collection, *Spinach Days*, was issued in the spring of 2000. He is former director of the creative writing program and John and Rebecca Moores Scholar at the University of Houston. Phillips's prizes include an Award in Literature from the American Academy of Arts and Letters. Three of his books have been named a Notable Book of the Year by the *New York Times Book Review*. He is poetry editor of *Texas Review* and a councilor of the Texas Institute of Letters.

JAMES RAGAN is the author of five books, *In the Talking Hours, Womb-Weary, The Hunger Wall, Lusions*, and *The World Shoulding I*, and the plays *Saints* and *Commedia* starring Raymond Burr. Ragan is director of the Graduate Professional Writing Program at the University of Southern California. Among other honors, he has received two Fulbright Professorships, the Emerson Poetry Prize, and a fellowship from the National Endowment for the Arts.

PAULETTE ROESKE holds degrees from Iowa, Northwestern, and the M.F.A. program at Warren Wilson. As a poet, she is published by the venerable LSU Press and has won many awards. Recent honors include an N.E.H. Fellowship, a Fulbright Scholarship, an Illinois Arts Council Fellowship, and a finalist in Ohio State University's 1997 fiction award. She has given readings of her work for PEN, and is herself the editor of the *Willow Review*.

MARTHA SERPAS is the author of a poetry collection, *Côte Blanche*. Her poems have appeared in literary journals, magazines, textbooks, and anthologies, including *Uncommonplace*, an anthology of Louisiana poets. She lectures in the community on the relationship between spiritual belief and literary works, and is active in the arts, literature, and religion section of the American Academy of Religion and in the Associated Writing Programs. She currently is an assistant professor of English at the University of Tampa.

R. T. SMITH was born in the District of Columbia and has lived in Georgia, North Carolina, Alabama, and Virginia. His family origins in the west of Ireland contribute to his interest in Irish literature and music, and he has received literature fellowships from the N.E.A., the Alabama Commission of the Arts, and Arts International. His most recent books are *Trespasser* in the States and *Split the Lark: Selected Poems* in Ireland. Another collection, *Messenger*, was published in 2001. He currently edits *Shenandoah* and lives in Rockbridge County, Virginia.

DAVID STARKEY is associate professor of English at North Central College in Naperville, Illinois, and in 1999 was Fulbright Professor of English at the University of Oulu in Finland. Over the past twelve years, more than 250 of his poems have appeared in a number of anthologies and in literary journals in America, Britain, Canada, Australia, and New Zealand. In addition to publishing several collections of poems with small presses, he has written a textbook, *Poetry Writing: Theme and Variations* and coedited, with Richard Guzman, an anthology of Chicago literature, *Smokestacks and Skyscrapers*.

LUCIEN STRYK's most recent books of poems are *And Still Birds Sing: New and Collected Poems* and *Where We Are: New and Selected Poems*. His most recent works of translation are *Zen Poetry: Let the Spring Breeze Enter, On Love and Barley: Haiku of Basho*, and *Triumph of the Sparrow: Zen Poems of Shinkishi Takahashi*. A recent collection of his essays and interviews is *The Awakened Self: Encounters with Zen*, and his 1968 edited book *World of the Buddha: An Introduction to Buddhist Literature* is still in print. Since retiring from Northern Illinois University, where he served as poet-in-residence and taught Asian literature for over thirty years, he gives readings and lectures in the United States and abroad. Two spoken albums of his work were brought out by Folkways Records, and his poems have been broadcast on PBS and the BBC in England.

MARK TURCOTTE is a Chippewa writer whose work has most appeared in *Poetry* and *Prairie Schooner*. He is the author of three poetry collections, including *Exploding Chippewas*. He lives in Fish Creek, Wisconsin. His poem "The Flower On" was chosen by the Poetry Society of America for inclusion in their "Poetry in Motion" project.

IVAN URQUIZA-VICENTE has been publishing works in Spanish—poetry, essays, philosophy, and fiction—since the age of eighteen. As an undergraduate at the University of Sevilla he was the recipient of the Dionisio A. Ramirez Prize for young poets in 1989, Ferria de juventud primer premio 1991, and published his first chapbook, *Cantos del Girasol*, in 1992. After a short career as a freelance political journalist he obtained an M.F.A. in creative writing from New York University and published two other poetry collections in Spanish: *Azucar* and *El Beso del la Carne*.

BRONISLAVA VOLKOVÁ was born in 1946 in Czechoslovakia. She grew up in Prague where she studied Slavic and Spanish linguistics and literature and received her Ph.D. at Charles University. She is currently a professor of Slavic languages and literatures at Indiana University as well as director of the Czech program and an adjunct professor of comparative literature. She is the author of eight books of Czech poetry, and her poems have appeared in English, Spanish, Polish, and French translations.

MICHAEL WATERS is professor of English at Salisbury State University on the Eastern Shore of Maryland. His six books of poetry include *Green Ash, Red Maple, Black Gum*; *Bountiful*; *The Burden Lifters*; and *Anniversary of the Air*. *New and Selected Poems* and his *Contemporary American Poetry* are forthcoming. He has been the recipient of a Fellowship in Creative Writing from the National Endowment for the Arts, three Individual Artist Awards from the Maryland State Arts Council, and two Pushcart Prizes.

CHARLES HARPER WEBB is professor of English at California State University—Long Beach, as well as a psychotherapist in private practice. He has previously published a novel, *The Wilderness Effect*, and a book of poems, *Reading the Water*, and has edited two other collections of poetry. Most recently, he won the Felix Pollack Prize in poetry at the University of Wisconsin Press for his book, *Liver*.

MARK WUNDERLICH is the author of *The Anchorage*, which won the Lambda Literary Award. The recipient of two fellowships from the Fine Arts Work Center in Provincetown, a Wallace Stegner Fellowship from Stanford University, and the Writers at Work Fellowship, he has published individual poems, essays, reviews, and interviews in the *Paris Review*, *Yale Review*, *Boston Review*, *Chicago Review*, *Fence*, and elsewhere. Wunderlich has taught at Stanford, San Francisco State University, Barnard College, and Ohio University. He currently lives in San Francisco.

Permissions

We are grateful to the authors who have given us permission to include previously unpublished work in this anthology. We also thank the authors, editors, and publishers who have given us permission to reprint poems.

David Baker, "Mercy," "Heavenly," and "The Puritan Way of Death" appear by permission of the author.

Jack Bedell, "*Les Mains du Bon Dieu*," appears by permission of the author. This poem originally appeared in *Connecticut Review* and subsequently in *What Passes for Love* (Texas Review Press, 2001) by Jack B. Bedell.

Marvin Bell, "The Hole in the Sea," appears by permission of the author. "The Book of the Dead Man (#13)" and "Sounds of the Resurrected Dead Man's Footsteps (#3)" are reprinted from *The Book of the Dead Man.*

J. J. Blickstein, "Vision of Salt & Water," first published in *Sundog*, appears here by permission of the author.

Bruce Bond, "Host," first published in *Radiography* (BOA Editions, 1997), appears here by permission of the author and BOA Editions. "Transparencies" appears here by permission of the author.

Darrell Bourque, "Durer's *Apollo*," appears by permission of the author. "Old Women Fishing from Bridges" is reprinted from *Plainsongs* (Cross-Cultural Communications, 1994) and appears here by permission of the author.

Gaylord Brewer, "Penance and the Work Week," appears by permission of the author. "Christ, the End," first published in *Santa Clara Review*, appears here by permission of the author. "Transport of the Dead," first published in *Poetry Wales*, appears here by permission of the author.

Maxine Chernoff, "God," appears here by permission of the author.

Martha Collins, "Epiphany" and "Pentecost," first published in *The Arrangement of Space* (Peregrine Smith, 1991), appear here by permission of the author and Peregrine Smith.

Nicole Cooley, "Resurrection," reprinted by permission of Louisiana State University Press from *Resurrection*, by Nicole Cooley. Copyright © 1996 by Nicole Cooley.

Peter Cooley, "For Jude the Obscure," "Vespers," and "Psalm before Sleep," appear by permission of the author.

Robert Dana, "Radiance," first appeared in the *Kenyon Review* and was subsequently reprinted from *Summer* (Anhinga Press). Copyright ©

Jarret Keene, "Exodus" and "God Lovingly Counterattacks" appear by permission of the author.

Carolyn Kizer, "*Dixit Insipiens,*" is reprinted from *Cool, Calm and Collected Poems* (Copper Canyon Press, 2002) and appears here by permission of the author and Copper Canyon Press.

Ko Won, "Jack in the Box," appears here by permission of the author.

Sydney Lea, "Still dark when we file like children out on the turf" and "Do not trust in these deceptive words:" from *Prayer for the Little City* (Scribner, 1991), are reprinted here by permission of the author.

Li-Young Lee, "A Table in the Wilderness," "Nativity," and "Little Round" first appeared in *Book of My Nights* (BOA Editions, 2001), and appear here by permission of the author and BOA Editions.

Peter Meinke, "Anthills," first appeared in *Scars* (University of Pittsburgh Press, 1996) and appears here by permission of the author and the University of Pittsburgh Press.

Leonard Nathan, "Quartet," is reprinted from *Tears of the Old Magician* (Orchises Press, 2003) and appears here by permission of the author and Orchises Press.

Richard Newman, "Theology," appears by permission of the author.

Linda Pastan, "A Short History of Judaic Thought in the Twentieth Century" and "The Apple Shrine" are reprinted from *Carnival Evening: New and Selected Poems 1968–1998* (W. W. Norton, 1999) and appear here by permission of W. W. Norton. "Muse" is reprinted from *The Last Uncle* (W. W. Norton, 2002) and appears here by permission of W. W. Norton.

Ricardo Pau-Llosa, "Segovia," first published in the *Journal* (fall/winter 1995), appears here by permission of the author. "Noah," first published in *Virginia Quarterly Review* (fall 1999), appears here by permission of the author. "The Hollow," first published in *Denver Quarterly* (summer 1995), appears here by permission of the author.

Saleem Peeradina, "Song of Surrender" and "Testament" appear by permission of the author.

Robert Phillips, "At the Summit" and "The Wounded Angel" copyright © 1986 by Robert Phillips.

James Ragan, "St. Jacob's Church of the Hanging Hand," is reprinted from *The Hunger Wall* (Grove Press, 1995) and appears here by permission of the author and Grove Press. "The Birth of God (from an Early Photograph)" is reprinted from *Lusions* (Grove Press, 1997) and appears here by permission of the author and Grove Press.

Paulette Roeske, "After the Funeral" from *Anvil, Clock and Last* by Paulette Roeske. Copyright © 2001 by Paulette Roeske. Reprinted with permission of Louisiana State University Press. "In the Theatre" from *Divine Attention* by Paulette Roeske. Copyright © 1995 by Paulette Roeske. Reprinted with permission of Louisiana State University Press.

Martha Serpas, "As If There Were Only One," first published in *Image:*

Further Readings

This list is by no means comprehensive, but it can provide a jumping-off point for future pursuits in religious and spiritual studies, whether in poetic or other forms. A particularly effective way of finding more relevant texts is to check any bibliographic or further or suggested readings information found in these books.

Ahlstrom, Sydney E. *A Religious History of the American People.* New Haven, Conn.: Yale University Press, 1974.

Barrows, Anita. *Rilke's Book of Hours: Love Poems to God.* New York: Riverhead Books, 1997.

Bloom, Harold. *The Book of J.* Trans. David Rosenberg. New York: Vintage/Random, 1991.

Chadwick, Henry. *The Early Church.* New York: Penguin, 1967.

Crossan, Dominic. *The Essential Jesus.* New York: HarperCollins, 1994.

Durkheim, Emile. *The Elementary Forms of the Religious Life.* New York: Free Press, 1965.

Eliade, Mircea. *Cosmos and History: The Myth of the Eternal Return.* Princeton, N.J.: Princeton University Press, 1954.

Freud, Sigmund. *Civilizations and Its Discontents.* New York: Norton, 1989.

Hartill, Rosemary, ed. *Writers Revealed: Eight Contemporary Novelists Talk about Faith, Religion and God.* New York: Peter Bedrick Books, 1989.

Hartz, Louis. *The Liberal Tradition in America.* New York: Harcourt Brace, 1991.

Hirshfield, Jane, ed. *Women in Praise of the Sacred.* New York: HarperPerennial Library, 1995.

Jacobsen, Thorkild. *The Treasures of Darkness: A History of Mesopotamian Religion.* New Haven, Conn.: Yale University Press, 1978.

Kazin, Alfred. *God and the American Writer.* New York: Alfred A. Knopf, 1997.

Lévi-Strauss, Claude. *The Savage Mind.* Chicago: University of Chicago Press, 1968.

MacLeish, Archibald. *J.B.* Boston: Houghton Mifflin, 1965.

Oden, Robert A. *The Bible without Theology.* Urbana, Ill.: University of Illinois Press, 2000.

Turner, Victor. *Forest of Symbols.* Ithaca, N.Y.: Cornell University Press, 1970.

Weber, Max. *The Protestant Ethic and the Spirit of Capitalism.* New York: Scribner's, 1980.

Zaleski, Philip, ed. *The Book of Heaven.* Oxford University Press, 2000.

Zaleski, Philip, series ed. *The Best Spiritual Writing.* San Francisco: HarperSanFrancisco (annual since 1998).

Index to Titles